The **MODERN
MULTI-COOKER
COOKBOOK**

# The **MODERN MULTI-COOKER** COOKBOOK

## 101 recipes for your Instant Pot®

**JENNY TSCHIESCHE**

Photography by **STEVE PAINTER**

RYLAND PETERS & SMALL
LONDON • NEW YORK

**Senior designer** Toni Kay
**Editors** Gillian Haslam and
Miriam Catley
**Production manager**
Gordana Simakovic
**Art director** Leslie Harrington
**Editorial director** Julia Charles
**Publisher** Cindy Richards

**Photography & prop styling**
Steve Painter
**Food stylist** Lucy McKelvie
**Indexer** Vanessa Bird

First published in 2018 by
Ryland Peters & Small
20–21 Jockey's Fields
London WC1R 4BW
and 341 E 116th St
New York NY 10029
www.rylandpeters.com

10 9 8 7 6 5 4 3 2 1

ISBN: 978-1-84975-973-1

Printed in China

A CIP record for this book is available
from the British Library. US Library of
Congress Cataloging-in-Publication
Data has been applied for.

**Notes:**
• Note that the 6-litre/quart Instant
Pot® LUX and Instant Pot® DUO
models of multi-cooker were used
for devising and testing the recipes
featured in this book, and preparing
them for the photography featured.
If you are using an alternative brand
of multi-cooker please refer closely
to the manufacturer's manual in order
to adjust the operating instructions
as appropriate for each recipe.
• Both British (Metric) and American
(Imperial plus US cups) measurements
are included in these recipes for your
convenience, however it is important
to work with one set of measurements
only and not alternate between the
two within a recipe.
• All spoon measurements are
level unless otherwise specified. A
teaspoon is 5 ml, a tablespoon is 15 ml.
• All eggs are medium (UK) or large
(US), unless specified as large, in
which case US extra-large should be
used. Uncooked or partially cooked
eggs should not be served to the very
old, frail, young children, pregnant
women or those with compromised
immune systems.

**Disclaimer:**
The views expressed in this book
are those of the author but they are
general views only. Ryland Peters &
Small hereby exclude all liability to the
extent permitted by law for any errors
or omissions in this book and for any
loss, damage or expense (whether
direct or indirect) suffered by a third
party relying on any information
contained in this book.

**Useful Terminology Used in Recipes:**

**QPR:** Quick Pressure Release
literally means you manually release
the pressure quickly by turning the
vent valve on the top of the machine
to open. Use a wooden spoon to do
this and make sure the vent is not
going to expel steam straight onto
a socket or any electrical equipment.

**NPR:** Natural Pressure Release refers
to allowing the pot to release built-up
pressure naturally. You'll know when
it's done because the pressure button
will pop back down.

**PIP:** Pot In Pot means cooking foods
in a pot inside your Instant Pot®.
This can be used not only to make
cakes, omelettes and meatloaves,
but also for cooking potatoes or
other vegetables at the same time
as the meal is cooking.

**Inner Pot:** This is the stainless steel
pot that you do all your cooking in.
It's durable and easily washed. I tend
to wash, dry and immediately replace
the pot so I don't have any mishaps.
People have been known to pour water
straight into the pot with no inner pot
there – that's a quick way to ruin your
Instant Pot®.

**Deglaze:** This is the term used to
mean that some liquid will be added
and a wooden spoon used to scrape
up any tasty bits from the bottom
of the pot. This is a necessary step
in many recipes to ensure that the
dish cooks through and doesn't stop
cooking or overheat due to food
sticking to the bottom of the pot.

# CONTENTS

# INTRODUCTION

Creating tasty and nutritious meals day after day is what we all aspire to, but it can become a chore. I'm a mum to two children, a health writer, nutritionist, speaker and presenter so, like many people, I'm spinning several plates. How I've wished for a magic gadget that would allow me to throw in a few ingredients and press a button, returning when the time is up to find a delicious meal, ready to eat. A gadget that would be easier and safer to use than an old-fashioned pressure cooker, faster than a slow cooker, yet producing slow-cooked textures and flavours. Reader, such a machine exists and it is called an Instant Pot®. This book will tell you how to use it and get the best from it, and I promise it will change your life (and no, I'm not sponsored by Instant Pot®!).

At its most basic, the Instant Pot® is an electric pressure cooker and slow cooker in one. This description underplays its abilities though, because the Instant Pot® can create the most incredible range of desserts, yogurts, porridge and risottos, too. With this one-pot way of cooking, once supper is in the pot, you can leave it unattended – it's silent, sturdy and very safe. There's a timer on the pot, too, so it can start and stop cooking at specified times, then keep your meal warm until you are ready to eat.

For this book, I've created a collection of recipes that you can recreate yourself without having to master any tricky culinary skills. The book is split into sections based on the type of dish. These are mostly family-size meals with a few exceptions, but even if you are not feeding a family, the bonus is that you can batch-cook meals and save portions in the fridge or freezer (you can even reheat meals from frozen).

The joy of writing this book has been discovering just how easy it is to create delicious and nutritious meals in such a hands-off way. The ingredients I cook with are the kind you will find in your local supermarket. From time to time I might use something from a specialist store, but it's now easy to purchase these ingredients online.

One additional benefit of this method of cooking is that many foods simply taste better – the flavours really shine through. The use of crushed tomatoes in a pasta dish or stew, for example, will make the dish taste sweet and have a great depth of flavour, complementing the vegetables served within the meal. Texturally this way of cooking can also help those who may be a little more particular about certain ingredients. Celery – not always a favourite ingredient – tastes much nicer when pressure cooked, while mushrooms really do absorb flavours. Onions also taste wonderfully sweet once pressure cooked.

Meat and fish textures are much softer using this method of cooking, too. I've worked with many families whose children won't eat meat or fish because they don't like the texture. Most of these children enjoy minced/ground meat so why not beef, lamb, salmon or chicken? A pressure-cooked stew, casserole, chowder or even a whole roast chicken results in meat or fish that simply melts in the mouth.

As far as extra equipment is concerned, I use the trivet that comes with the Instant Pot® to rest fish, vegetables and eggs on, while cooking another element of the whole dish underneath the trivet. I also bought a silicone trivet, a cake 'pan' and steaming basket, as well as a heatproof 1-litre/35-oz. glass Pyrex bowl and a small loaf pan. Scales and measuring jugs/cups are handy, particularly for getting ratios of pasta or rice to water correct. This is one area where it pays to be precise, otherwise you'll end up with a sloppy meal with too much liquid or a burnt meal that simply won't cook because the Instant Pot® will overheat.

If you are new to this way of cooking, I recommend you start by following the recipes, then once you've got your confidence, you can experiment with your own flavours and preferences. The recipe methods use abbreviations and these are explained on page 4, so refer back to them as necessary.

# BREAKFASTS

# GRAIN-FREE BIRCHER MUESLI

20 g/2 tablespoons ground
   flaxseeds/linseeds
25 g/3 tablespoons pumpkin
   seeds
25 g/2½ tablespoons chia seeds
60 g/½ cup sunflower seeds
40 g/scant ½ cup ground
   almonds
2 eating apples, cored and grated
1 teaspoon ground cinnamon
¼ teaspoon ground ginger
200 ml/¾ cup coconut milk
200 g/¾ cup apple purée
   (see page 12)

TO SERVE
Greek yogurt
yacon or maple syrup

Serves 3

*A great way to enjoy a filling grain-free
porridge alternative for breakfast.*

Place all the ingredients in a 1-litre/35-oz
heatproof glass bowl and stir well.

Place 250 ml/1 cup water in the multi-cooker.
Place the trivet in the inner pot. Pop the glass
bowl on top.

Secure the lid in place and set to Manual
or High Pressure for 3 minutes. At the end of
cooking, use the QPR method (see page 4).

Serve each portion topped with a spoonful
of yogurt and a drizzle of yacon or maple syrup.

# SIMPLE DAIRY-FREE, GLUTEN-FREE PORRIDGE

70 g/¾ cup gluten-free
  porridge/rolled oats
  (or 35 g/¼ cup oats and
  35 g/¼ cup buckwheat
  or quinoa flakes)
250 ml/1 cup rice, almond
  or coconut milk

Serves 2

*This simple porridge is fairly flexible in terms of the grains used. I tend to combine protein-rich buckwheat or quinoa with oats as both have quite a strong flavour by comparison to oats. You could, however, make the porridge with just buckwheat or just quinoa flakes if you wished.*

Put the porridge/rolled oats and buckwheat or quinoa flakes, if using, and milk in a heatproof glass bowl and stir.

Place 500 ml/2 cups water in the multi-cooker and add the trivet. Place the glass bowl on top.

Secure the lid in place and set to Manual or High Pressure for 10 minutes. At the end of cooking, use the QPR method (see page 4).

**Note:** you can double this recipe to serve 4 people.

# APPLE PURÉE

8 large eating apples, peeled,
  cored and cut into wedges
70 ml/5 tablespoons apple juice
¾ teaspoon ground cinnamon
¼ teaspoon ground cloves

Serves 6

*Apple purée is great in the bircher recipe on page 11. It also makes a quick and tasty dessert when served with yogurt and sprinkled with cinnamon.*

Put all the ingredients into the multi-cooker. Secure the lid in place and set to Manual or High Pressure for 6 minutes. At the end of cooking, use the QPR method (see page 4).

Pop the mixture into the bowl of a food processor or use a stick blender to blend to a smooth purée.

# RHUBARB AND RASPBERRY COMPOTE

**5 sticks of rhubarb, chopped
into 3-cm/1¹/₄-in. pieces**
**400 g/4 cups raspberries**
**¹/₈ teaspoon stevia powder**

TO SERVE
**Greek yogurt**

Serves 8

*A wonderfully red and deliciously fruity
compote to serve over Greek yogurt.*

Put 200 ml/³/₄ cup water into the base of the multi-cooker and
add the trivet. Place the fruit in a 1-litre/35-oz heatproof glass bowl
and sprinkle over the stevia. Cover the bowl with foil and place on
top of the trivet.

   Secure the lid in place and set to Manual or High Pressure for
20 minutes. At the end of cooking, use the QPR method (see page 4).

   Remove the foil and once the compote has cooled a little, place
it in the bowl of a food processor and process to a slightly chunky
compote texture. Serve over Greek yogurt.


# RASPBERRY CRISP

**335 g/3¹/₄ cups fresh or frozen
raspberries (defrosted if frozen)**
**¹/₈ teaspoon stevia powder**
**60 g/¹/₂ cup chopped roasted
hazelnuts**
**60 g/²/₃ cup ground almonds**
**40 g/¹/₂ cup quinoa flakes**
**50 g/3 tablespoons ghee**
**2 teaspoons date syrup
or honey**

Serves 4–6

*Based on the more traditional apple crisp, here I've
used juicy raspberries and a crunchy topping made
of nuts and quinoa flakes.*

Place the raspberries in a 1-litre/35-oz heatproof glass bowl.
Sprinkle over the stevia and mash the raspberries down with the
back of a fork.

   In a separate bowl, mix the chopped hazelnuts, almonds, quinoa
flakes, ghee and date syrup or honey. Spoon this mixture over the
raspberries. Cover the bowl with foil.

   Place 200 ml/³/₄ cup water in the inner pot of the multi-cooker.
Put the trivet inside the pot, then the glass dish on top.

   Secure the lid in place, then set to Manual or High Pressure for
10 minutes. At the end of cooking, use the NPR method (see page 4).

   Enjoy as is or with Greek yogurt or coconut milk yogurt.

# SPELT BANANA BREAD

**140 g/1 ¼ sticks soft butter**
**95 g/½ cup coconut sugar**
**2 eggs**
**2 bananas, mashed**
**135 g/1 cup wholemeal/**
   **whole-wheat spelt flour**
**2½ teaspoons baking powder**

a 15-cm/6-inch circular
   springform cake pan or
   a 15 x 8 x 5-cm/6 x 3¼ x 2-inch
   non-stick mini loaf pan

Makes 1 loaf

*A deliciously moist banana bread*
*made with spelt flour.*

In a bowl, mix together the butter and sugar.
Add the eggs and mashed banana and stir. In a
separate bowl, mix the flour and baking powder.
Add the dry mixture to the wet mixture and
combine. Pour into the cake or loaf pan.

Place the cake or loaf pan on the trivet. Add
450 ml/scant 2 cups water to the multi-cooker,
then lower the trivet and cake or loaf pan into the
inner pot.

Secure the lid in place and set to Manual
or High Pressure for 30 minutes. At the end of
cooking, use the NPR method (see page 4) for
15 minutes, then use QPR. Be careful when you
remove the lid not to drip any liquid onto the loaf.
If necessary, dab off water using paper towels.

Allow the loaf to cool a little before removing
from the pan and leaving on a wire rack to cool
completely. Serve in thick slices.

# GRAIN-FREE BREAD

50 g/½ cup macadamia nuts
20 g/2 tablespoons ground
    flaxseeds/linseeds
15 g/1¾ tablespoons coconut
    flour
½ teaspoon bicarbonate of/
    baking soda
¼ teaspoon salt
20 g/4 teaspoons ghee, coconut
    oil or butter
1½ teaspoons honey or maple
    syrup
½ teaspoon apple cider vinegar
3 eggs

a 15 x 8 x 5-cm/6 x 3¼ x 2-inch
non-stick mini loaf pan

Makes 1 loaf

*This is a delicious and nutritious fibre-rich loaf made without grains. As well as being a great breakfast bread, it is delicious served with the chicken liver pâté recipe on page 41.*

In a food processor, grind the nuts, flaxseeds/linseeds, coconut flour, bicarbonate of/baking soda and salt. Add the ghee, oil or butter, the honey or syrup, vinegar and eggs. Process again to a batter. Pour the mixture into a mini loaf pan.

Place the loaf pan on the trivet. Add 450 ml/scant 2 cups water to the multi-cooker, then lower the trivet and loaf pan into the inner pot.

Secure the lid in place and set to Manual or High Pressure for 30 minutes. At the end of cooking, use the QPR method (see page 4).

Allow the loaf to cool a little, then remove from the loaf pan and leave on a wire rack to cool completely.

SOUPS

# CARROT AND GINGER SOUP

1 tablespoon olive oil or butter
2 onions, diced
1 celery stalk, sliced into
    2-cm/³/₄-in. pieces
1 tablespoon crushed garlic
1 tablespoon freshly grated ginger
1½ teaspoons ground cumin
½ teaspoon ground coriander
1½ teaspoons salt
3 medium tomatoes,
    cut into quarters
500 g/1 lb. 2 oz. carrots, peeled
    and sliced into 2-cm/³/₄-in.
    pieces
150 ml/²/₃ cup coconut milk

Serves 4

*This is a simple soup that is packed full of flavour. The tomatoes in the recipe give a layer of tangy sweetness to the soup.*

Press the Sauté button on the multi-cooker. Add the oil or butter to the pot. When hot or melted, add the onions and celery and stir. Cook for 3–4 minutes, then add the garlic, ginger, cumin, coriander and salt and stir to combine.

Add the tomatoes and carrots and stir again to deglaze the pan (see page 4). Add the coconut milk and 250 ml/1 cup water and stir.

Secure the lid in place and set to Manual or High Pressure for 6 minutes. At the end of cooking, use the NPR method (see page 4) for 7 minutes, then use QPR. Use a stick blender or food processor to process the soup to your desired consistency, then reheat and serve.

# CURRIED CHICKPEA SOUP

45 ml/3 tablespoons olive oil
15 g/¹/₃ cup freshly chopped
    coriander/cilantro
2 onions, finely chopped
2 garlic cloves, finely chopped
1 teaspoon finely chopped
    fresh ginger
10 cherry tomatoes
2 tablespoons tomato paste
½ teaspoon ground cinnamon
1 teaspoon ground cumin
½ teaspoon ground coriander
1 teaspoon ground turmeric
220 g/1¹/₃ cups dried chickpeas,
    soaked overnight in water,
    drained and rinsed the next day
1 vegetable stock cube or
    1 tablespoon vegetable stock
    paste (see page 31)

Serves 4

*Using dried legumes and pulses is a really cost-effective way of producing nourishing family meals. Here dried chickpeas require overnight soaking in water.*

Press the Sauté button on the multi-cooker. Add the olive oil to the pot. When hot, add the coriander/cilantro, onions, garlic and ginger and sauté, stirring constantly, for about 3–4 minutes.

Add the cherry tomatoes and tomato paste. Stir again for about 2 minutes to deglaze the pan (see page 4), then add the cinnamon, cumin, coriander and turmeric. As soon as these are absorbed into the dish, add the chickpeas, stock cube or vegetable stock paste and 500 ml/2 cups water.

Secure the lid in place and set to Manual or High Pressure for 20 minutes. At the end of cooking, use the NPR method (see page 4) to let the flavours mellow. Good served with natural yogurt and a sprinkling of chopped red onion over the top.

# CAULIFLOWER, WHITE SWEET POTATO AND CHORIZO SOUP

1 tablespoon olive oil
2 onions, halved and sliced
100 g/3½ oz. chorizo, chopped
  into bite-sized pieces
1 large cauliflower, chopped into
  very large pieces
650 g/1 lb. 7 oz. white sweet
  potatoes, peeled and chopped
  into 3 x 3-cm/1¼ x 1¼-in. cubes
200 g/7 oz. passata/strained
  tomatoes
1 tablespoon salt
1 tablespoon pomegranate
  molasses or 3 tablespoons
  grated cheese, to garnish

Serves 6

*This is a mellow combination of satisfying salty and sweet flavours. White sweet potatoes are increasingly available in Asian stores and supermarkets, but if you cannot find them simply use orange sweet potatoes.*

Press the Sauté button on the multi-cooker. Add the oil to the pot. When hot, add the onions and chorizo and cook, stirring, for 4 minutes. Add all the other ingredients except the molasses or cheese, plus 750 ml/3 cups water.

Secure the lid in place and set to Manual or High Pressure for 5 minutes. At the end of cooking, use the NPR method (see page 4) for at least 20 minutes or until the valve pops back down.

Serve in deep bowls with a drizzle of pomegranate molasses over the top. Alternatively, top with some grated cheese.

# CAULIFLOWER AND BACON SOUP

1 tablespoon ghee or butter
2 onions, chopped
5 slices of streaky bacon, chopped
1 large cauliflower, chopped
  into large florets
1 tablespoon vegetable stock
  paste (see page 31) or
  1 vegetable stock cube
1 teaspoon tamari or coconut
  aminos

Serves 4

*A classic combination - cauliflower and bacon are just made for each other.*

Press the Sauté button on the multi-cooker. Add the ghee or butter to the pot. When melted, add the onions and bacon. Cook for about 4 minutes, stirring regularly, then add the cauliflower, stock paste or cube, tamari or coconut aminos and 800 ml/3⅓ cups water.

Secure the lid in place and set to Manual or High Pressure for 6 minutes. At the end of cooking, use the QPR method (see page 4), then process using a stick blender or a food processor, reheat and serve.

# BUTTERNUT SQUASH, SPINACH AND CHICKPEA SOUP

1 tablespoon ghee or coconut oil

1 onion, halved and sliced

350 g/12 oz. butternut squash (peeled weight), chopped into 2 x 2-cm/³/₄ x ³/₄-in. cubes

3 tablespoons mild korma paste

¹/₂ teaspoon salt

freshly squeezed juice of ¹/₂ small lemon

1 x 400-g/14-oz. can chickpeas, drained and rinsed (240 g/8¹/₂ oz. drained weight)

1 x 400-ml/14-fl. oz. can coconut milk

175 g/6 oz. frozen spinach

300 ml/1¹/₄ cups vegetable stock, made with 1 teaspoon vegetable stock paste (see page 31), or ¹/₂ vegetable stock cube and 300 ml/1¹/₄ cups water

Serves 4

*This is a very satisfying soup with a mild yet warming curry flavour.*

Press the Sauté button on the multi-cooker. Add the ghee or coconut oil to the pot. When hot, add the onion and stir until translucent. Add the butternut squash and stir. Then stir in the korma paste, salt, lemon juice, chickpeas, coconut milk, spinach and stock, being sure to deglaze the pot at this stage (see page 4).

Secure the lid in place and set to Manual or High Pressure for 15 minutes. At the end of cooking, use the QPR method (see page 4).

# CHICKPEA, POTATO AND BACON SOUP

1 tablespoon butter

1 onion, thinly sliced

130 g/5 oz. chopped bacon
   or lardons

2 carrots, sliced into discs

1 courgette/zucchini, thickly
   sliced into discs

350 g/12 oz. potatoes, peeled
   and cubed

1 x 400-g/14-oz. can chickpeas,
   drained and rinsed

500 ml/2 cups beef stock or
   broth (if not salted, add
   extra salt to taste)

Serves 4

*The chickpeas and potatoes give this soup
a creaminess that makes it taste more luxurious
than its basic ingredients might suggest.*

Press Sauté on the multi-cooker. Add the butter to the pot.
When melted, add the onion, bacon, carrots and courgette/
zucchini. Stir for about 5 minutes until the onion is almost
transparent. Add the potatoes, chickpeas and beef stock
and deglaze the pot (see page 4).

   Secure the lid in place and set to Manual or High Pressure
for 4 minutes. At the end of cooking, use the QPR method
(see page 4). Serve in bowls with slices of buttered toasted
sourdough or grain-free bread (see page 19).

# SAM'S SOUP

1 tablespoon ghee or butter

1 onion, chopped

3 carrots, chopped

75-g/2$\frac{1}{2}$-oz. pack diced pancetta

1$\frac{1}{2}$ stock cubes or 1$\frac{1}{2}$ tablespoons
   vegetable stock paste
   (see page 31)

400 g/14 oz. (drained weight)
   canned chickpeas (which
   means more than one can
   will be required)

Serves 4

*A recipe created by my ravenous son on a whim
one afternoon. Now, of course, it is his favourite
soup and none of my soups are as good as his!*

Press the Sauté button on the multi-cooker. Add the ghee
or butter to the pot. When melted, add the onion, carrots and
pancetta. Stir for about 5 minutes until the onion is almost
translucent. Add the stock cube or vegetable stock paste
and a little water to deglaze the pot (see page 4). Then add
750 ml/3$\frac{1}{4}$ cups water and the chickpeas.

   Secure the lid in place and set to Manual or High Pressure
for 2 minutes. At the end of cooking, use the QPR method
(see page 4). Use a stick blender or food processer to blend
to your desired consistency, then reheat and serve.

# FRENCH ONION SOUP

2 tablespoons butter
1 teaspoon olive oil
4 onions, halved and sliced
135 ml/²⁄₃ cup white wine
3 garlic cloves
2 sprigs of fresh thyme
2 tablespoons vegetable stock
 paste (see below) or
 2 vegetable stock cubes

TO SERVE
Worcestershire sauce (gluten-
 free, if you wish), grated
 Parmesan or pecorino and
 fresh thyme leaves

Serves 4

*The ingredients for this classic soup are cost-effective,
but the depth of flavour comes from cooking the onions
for as long as it takes for them to become brown and sweet.*

Press the Sauté button on the multi-cooker. Add the butter and
oil to the pot. When the butter has melted, add the onions and stir
regularly until they are soft and browning. If they start to stick to the
base of the pot, use a little wine to deglaze (see page 4). Add more
wine and the garlic and stir until the wine is almost evaporated. Add
the thyme, stock paste or cubes and 1 litre/1 quart water and stir.

Secure the lid in place and set to Manual or High Pressure for
7 minutes. At the end of cooking, use the NPR method (see page 4).
Add a little Worcestershire Sauce and grated cheese before serving,
and scatter over some fresh thyme leaves.

# VEGETABLE STOCK PASTE

160 g/5½ oz. vegan cheese
 or pecorino, grated
3 garlic cloves, finely chopped
200 g/7 oz. celery heart, very
 finely chopped
3 tomatoes, very finely chopped
130 g/4½ oz. mushrooms,
 very finely chopped
2 large leeks, finely chopped
2 carrots, finely chopped
1 large onion, finely chopped
2 tenderstem broccoli/
 broccolini, chopped
1 teaspoon ground turmeric
1 tablespoon dried oregano
1 tablespoon freshly chopped
 parsley
55 ml/3½ tablespoons apple
 cider vinegar
2 tablespoons olive oil
100 g/½ cups salt

Makes 2.5 x 500 ml/18 fl. oz. jars

*This is used in many of the recipes in this book as I prefer
to use stock paste to cubes as I know what's gone into
homemade paste. In all the recipes where stock paste or
cube is called for, you can use 1 stock cube or 1 tablespoon
stock paste interchangeably. Thanks to my friend and
Instant Pot® expert Maria for the basis of this recipe.*

The quickest way to prepare this stock is to blitz the cheese, garlic
and vegetables in a food processor to reduce the amount of fine
chopping required. Once you have the base, simply put this in the
multi-cooker, along with all the remaining ingredients, secure the lid
in place, then set to Manual or High Pressure for 10 minutes. At the
end of cooking, use the QPR method (see page 4).

When cool, blitz again in the food processor to a paste.
Place in sterilized glass jars and seal the lids, then store in the fridge
for up to 6 weeks or in the freezer (leave room for expansion in the
jars if freezing).

# DAIRY-FREE FISH CHOWDER

2 shallots, sliced using a mandolin
   on level 1
½ large bulb of fennel, sliced
   using a mandolin on level 1
1 medium sweet potato, peeled
   and diced
10 mushrooms, quartered
1 tablespoon freshly chopped
   flat-leaf parsley
½ teaspoon salt
400-ml/14-fl. oz. can coconut
   milk
300-g/10½-oz. pack fish pie mix

Serves 2–3

*The soup is cooked first and the bite-sized pieces of fish added afterwards to ensure both are cooked perfectly and come together in harmony at the end.*

Put the shallots, fennel, sweet potato, mushrooms, parsley, salt and about 220 ml/1 cup coconut milk into the multi-cooker. Secure the lid in place and set to Manual or High Pressure for 3 minutes. At the end of cooking, use the QPR method (see page 4), then open the lid.

Press the Sauté button and add the fish plus the remaining coconut milk. Heat for about 3–4 minutes until the fish is just cooked through (it should start to flake apart). Serve immediately.

# BONE BROTH

500 g/1 lb. 2 oz. chicken, turkey,
   beef or lamb bones, ideally
   organic
3 carrots
3 celery stalks
1 onion
a couple of bay leaves
some black peppercorns
1 tablespoon apple cider vinegar
3 drops of fish sauce

Serves 4

*Bone broths provide protein and minerals. These can support the body's natural detoxification process, improve iron levels and aid digestive health, too. Use a chicken carcase, or buy some bones from your local butcher (you can use turkey, beef or lamb bones, too). Ideally choose organic bones. You need at least 500 g/1 lb. 2 oz.*

Put the bones into the multi-cooker, then add in all the other ingredients. Add water to the pot, roughly up to the 4-litre/1 gallon mark.

Secure the lid in place and set to Manual or High Pressure for 120 minutes. At the end of cooking, use the NPR method (see page 4).

Strain the broth using a colander. Store the broth in sterilized glass jars or in a glass bowl in the fridge. A layer of fat will rise to the surface – skim this off once it hardens. The broth can also be frozen for future use (leave a little room for expansion in the jars if freezing).

# CHESTNUT AND VEGETABLE SOUP

**1 tablespoon olive oil**
**1 onion, chopped**
**2 celery stalks, sliced**
**1 large carrot, chopped**
**1 courgette/zucchini, chopped**
**250 g/9 oz. chestnut purée**
**150 g/2 cups chopped mushrooms**
**750 ml/3¼ cups vegetable stock**
  **or 2 tablespoons**
  **vegetable stock paste (see**
  **page 31) plus 750 ml/3¼ cups**
  **water**
**freshly chopped flat-leaf parsley**
**salt and freshly ground**
  **black pepper**

Serves 4

*Nothing says 'autumn' more than this soup! This is the perfect comforting soup to return home to after a walk in the countryside.*

Press the Sauté button on the multi-cooker. Add the oil to the pot. Allow it to heat a little, then add the onion, celery, carrot and courgette/zucchini. Stir for about 5 minutes. Add the chestnut purée, mushrooms and stock and deglaze the pan (see page 4).

Secure the lid in place and set to Manual or High Pressure for 4 minutes. At the end of cooking, use the QPR method (see page 4). Allow to cool a little, then use a food processor or stick blender to blend to your desired consistency, then reheat. Season to taste.

Serve in bowls with slices of buttered toasted sourdough or Grain-free Bread (see page 19).

# SPLIT PEA AND BACON SOUP

1 tablespoon olive oil
1 large onion, chopped
2 celery stalks, finely chopped
2 carrots, finely chopped
4 slices of streaky bacon,
    chopped into small pieces
1/2 teaspoon ground cumin
1 vegetable stock cube or
    1 teaspoon vegetable stock
    paste (see page 31)
340 g/1³/₄ cups split green peas,
    well rinsed

Serves 4–6

*This is such a comforting soup and a great way of using up the vegetables left in the fridge at the end of the week.*

Press the Sauté button on the multi-cooker. Add the oil to the pot. When hot, add the vegetables and bacon. Stir for about 5 minutes until the onion is just becoming translucent. Add the cumin and stock cube or paste and stir well. Add the split peas and 1 litre/1 quart water and deglaze the pot (see page 4).

Secure the lid in place and set to Manual or High Pressure for 10 minutes. At the end of cooking, use the NPR method (see page 4) and serve warm.

# VEGETABLE AND BACON SOUP

1 tablespoon olive oil,
    avocado oil, butter or ghee
2 large leeks, sliced and washed
    thoroughly
2 carrots, peeled and diced
130 g/1 cup chopped bacon
    or lardons
2 potatoes (each about the size
    of a medium jacket potato),
    peeled and diced
generous 1/2 teaspoon salt
1/2 teaspoon dried thyme
1 bay leaf
200 g/2 cups grated/shredded
    cheese
freshly cracked black pepper

Serves 4

*This is one of those meals you'll be thankful for after a hard day when you really cannot be bothered to make a whole meal. It's a very simple but flavoursome soup.*

Press the Sauté button on the multi-cooker. Add the oil, butter or ghee to the pot. Leave for a couple of minutes to heat or melt, then add the leeks, carrots and bacon. Stir for about 8–10 minutes until the leeks are soft. Add the potatoes, salt, thyme, bay leaf and 500 ml/2 cups water and deglaze the pot (see page 4).

Secure the lid in place and set to Manual or High Pressure for 6 minutes. At the end of cooking, use the QPR method (see page 4). Serve in bowls with the grated/shredded cheese and some freshly cracked black pepper over the top.

# LIGHT BITES AND
# SPEEDY SUPPERS

# CARROT AND CASHEW HUMMUS

4 medium carrots
(about 200 g/7 oz. in total)
1 x 400-g/14-oz. can chickpeas,
drained and rinsed
2 tablespoons extra virgin olive oil
1 tablespoon cashew butter
1 teaspoon raw honey
1 teaspoon water
1 teaspoon ground cumin
½ garlic clove, peeled
salt and freshly ground
black pepper

Serves 6

*This fragrant hummus is a hit with younger palates
due to its warming spices and naturally sweet flavour.
It's delicious served with fresh vegetable crudités.*

Place 250 ml/1 cup water in the base of the multi-cooker, then
add the trivet to the inner pot. Peel, top and tail the carrots and
place on the trivet.

Secure the lid in place and set to Manual or High Pressure for
7 minutes. At the end of cooking, use the QPR method (see page 4).

Transfer the carrots to a food processor. Add all the remaining
ingredients and process to a hummus consistency. Season to taste.

# CHICKEN LIVER PÂTÉ

2 tablespoons butter or ghee
1 onion, chopped
75 g/2½ oz. cubed pancetta
400 g/14 oz. chicken livers,
trimmed
200 g/7 oz. mushrooms,
cut into quarters
1 tablespoon tamari or coconut
aminos
2 tablespoons red wine
salt and freshly ground
black pepper

Serves 10

*Chicken liver pâté is probably the 'safest' way to introduce
those who are wary of offal to something new and tasty.
It's a cost-effective, nutrient-rich dish and can be served
just cooled with a salad or chopped vegetables.*

Press the Sauté button on the multi-cooker and add the butter
or ghee to the pot. When melted, add the onion. Stir until soft, then
add the pancetta and livers. Brown the livers a little, then add the
mushrooms, tamari or coconut aminos and red wine, ensuring you
deglaze the pan at this stage (see page 4).

Secure the lid in place and set to Manual or High Pressure for
0 minutes. At the end of cooking, use the NPR method (see page 4).

Transfer the mixture to a food processor and process to a very
smooth consistency. Season to taste and process again. Leave to
cool a little, then enjoy. It will keep in an airtight container in the
fridge for 3 days.

# SWEET POTATO AND PANCETTA FRITTATA

**100 g/3½ oz. diced pancetta**
**1 medium sweet potato,**
 **peeled**
**1 small onion**
**8 eggs**
**½ teaspoon dried mixed herbs**
**¼ teaspoon garlic powder**
**¼ teaspoon salt**

a 20-cm/8-in. round silicone
 cake pan

Serves 2

*This exceptionally tasty savoury slice
makes for a delicious brunch, but once
cooled it is fantastically portable for
packed lunches or as part of a picnic.*

Press the Sauté button on the multi-cooker.
Add the pancetta to the pot and sauté until
cooked. Remove from the pot and place in the
base of the silicone cake pan.

Finely chop the sweet potato and onion in a
food processor. Add the eggs, herbs, garlic powder
and salt to the food processor and process again.
Pour this mixture over the top of the cooked
pancetta in the cake pan. Pour 250 ml/1 cup
water into the multi-cooker and deglaze the pan
(see page 4). Place the cake pan on the trivet and
lower into the multi-cooker.

Secure the lid in place and set to Manual
or High Pressure for 30 minutes. At the end of
cooking, use the QPR method (see page 4). You
may need to dab away any excess liquid on the
frittata using paper towels.

The frittata can be sliced and served warm
or cold. It will keep in an airtight container in
the fridge for 3 days.

# SPINACH AND SALMON EGG CUPS

¼ teaspoon olive oil

4 large eggs, beaten in a bowl

2 blocks of frozen spinach, defrosted (about 60 g/2 oz. frozen weight in total)

100 g/3½ oz. smoked salmon, thinly sliced or shredded

salt and freshly ground black pepper

4 ramekins

Serves 4

*These little ramekins of creamy egg and salty salmon with delicious and nutritious spinach are a real treat.*

Using a pastry brush, brush the insides of the four ramekins evenly with the oil.

To the bowl of beaten eggs, add the defrosted spinach and salmon, then season with salt and pepper. Pour the mixture evenly into the greased ramekins. Place 250 ml/1 cup water in the base of the inner pot. Add the trivet on top and place the ramekins on top of the trivet.

Secure the lid in place and set to Manual or High Pressure for 6 minutes. At the end of cooking, use the QPR method (see page 4) and serve immediately. The eggs may have risen during cooking, but they'll soon retract back into the ramekins.

# SALMON SUPPER WITH SWEET POTATOES

2 medium sweet potatoes, peeled and cubed

2 salmon fillets

1 x 200-g/7-oz. pack mixed vegetables for steaming (such as French/green beans, tenderstem broccoli/broccolini and asparagus)

1 teaspoon olive oil

salt and freshly ground black pepper

1 tablespoon butter

Serves 2

*Salmon is such a popular fish and is so easy to cook in a multi-cooker. This meal for two is a very straightforward dish that will surprise you with its simplicity and speed to plate.*

Place 250 ml/1 cup water in the multi-cooker. Put the sweet potato cubes into the water. Add the trivet and place the fish and mixed vegetables on the trivet. Drizzle the oil over the fish and vegetables and season with salt and pepper.

Secure the lid in place and set to Manual or High Pressure for 2 minutes. At the end of cooking, use the QPR method (see page 4). Remove the trivet, drain the sweet potatoes and serve the fish and vegetables with the sweet potatoes and the butter shared between the two plates.

1 tablespoon ghee

1 onion, chopped

approx. 20 French/green beans, topped, tailed and chopped into 1-cm/½-in. lengths

2 garlic cloves, crushed

1 green chilli/chile, finely chopped

1 teaspoon ground turmeric

¾ teaspoon ground cumin

1 teaspoon smoked paprika

1 teaspoon nigella/black onion seeds

¾ teaspoon salt

250 g/1½ cups basmati rice

4 blocks of frozen spinach (about 120 g/4 oz. frozen weight in total)

300–400 g/10½–14 oz. smoked salmon, cut into strips (or buy smoked salmon 'scraps' from your fishmonger)

4 eggs, hard-boiled/cooked, shelled and quartered

Serves 4

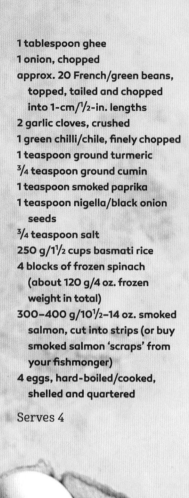

# SMOKED SALMON KEDGEREE

*Whilst traditional kedgeree is made with smoked haddock and without added vegetables, I've switched things up a little by adding in beans and spinach and serving with smoked salmon. It's a very tasty alternative to the traditional version.*

Press the Sauté button on the multi-cooker and add the ghee to the pot. When melted, add the onion, beans, garlic and chilli/chile. Stir constantly for about 4–5 minutes. Then add the spices, salt and rice. Stir well. Add the spinach and 320 ml/ 11 fl. oz. water to the multi-cooker and deglaze the pot (see page 4).

Secure the lid in place and set to Rice for 12 minutes. At the end of cooking, use the QPR method (see page 4). Serve with strips of smoked salmon and quartered hard-boiled/cooked eggs on top.

# COD IN PARMA HAM WITH LEMON BUTTER AND VEGETABLES

2 thick and chunky cod fillets
6 slices of Parma ham or
    prosciutto
1 tablespoon salted butter
½ head of cauliflower, chopped
    into medium florets
10 spears of asparagus,
    woody ends snapped off
3 mushrooms, halved
freshly squeezed juice of
    ½ lemon, plus lemon
    wedges to serve
1 tablespoon olive oil
salt and freshly ground
    black pepper

Serves 2

*The ham combines deliciously with the buttery cod in this dish. It's a whole meal served with the vegetables that are all cooked in the pot at the same time.*

Wrap each of the cod fillets in three slices of Parma or prosciutto ham.

Press the Sauté button on the multi-cooker. Add the butter and cauliflower and stir. When the butter begins to turn brown, add the asparagus and mushrooms and stir, then rest the ham-wrapped fish on top. Drizzle over the lemon juice and oil, then sprinkle over salt and pepper to taste.

Secure the lid in place and set to Manual or High Pressure for 2 minutes. At the end of cooking, use the QPR method (see page 4). Serve immediately, with lemon wedges on the side.

# SMOKED HADDOCK WITH FENNEL AND MUSHROOMS

1 tablespoon olive oil
1 fennel bulb, very finely chopped
    (reserve the feathery fronds
    to garnish)
8 medium mushrooms, cut into
    quarters
10 cherry tomatoes, cut in half
2 chunky smoked haddock fillets
lemon wedges, to serve

Serves 2

*A light, but flavoursome fish dish, and great for a quick and easy meal (photo on page 2).*

Press the Sauté button on the multi-cooker and add the oil. When hot, add the fennel and stir for about 5 minutes until softened. Add the mushrooms and tomatoes and stir, then lay the fillets of fish on top.

Secure the lid in place and set to Manual or High Pressure for 1 minute. At the end of cooking, use the NPR method (see page 4). Serve with lemon wedges and garnish with chopped feathery fennel fronds.

1½ tablespoons olive oil

2 small onions or 1 large onion, halved and thickly sliced

2 carrots, peeled, sliced into quarters lengthways and chopped into 1-cm/½-in. pieces

500 g/1 lb. 2 oz. organic minced/ ground beef

10 chestnut mushrooms, halved

400 g/14 oz. passata/strained tomatoes

1 tablespoon tamari or coconut aminos

2 tablespoons tomato paste

1½ teaspoons dried oregano

1 vegetable stock cube or 1 tablespoon vegetable stock paste (see page 31)

150 g/5½ oz. wholegrain spelt spaghetti, snapped in half to ensure even cooking

grated Parmesan, to serve

Serves 4

# ALL-IN-ONE SPAGHETTI BOLOGNESE

*This is one of those dishes that so many people love. Cooking the pasta in with the sauce is a real time-saver. This recipe uses wholegrain spelt spaghetti which adds great flavour.*

Press the Sauté button on the multi-cooker and add the oil. When hot, add the onions and carrots. Stir for about 5 minutes until the onions become translucent. Add the beef and stir to break it up and ensure even cooking.

When the beef has browned, add the mushrooms, passata/ strained tomatoes, tamari or coconut aminos, tomato paste, oregano and vegetable stock cube or paste, plus 300 ml/1¼ cups water. Deglaze the pot (see page 4), then push the halved spaghetti into the liquid, ensuring it is completely covered by the liquid.

Secure the lid in place and set to Manual or High Pressure for 7 minutes. At the end of cooking, use the QPR method (see page 4). Serve immediately, with grated Parmesan cheese if you wish.

1½ tablespoons olive oil

2 small onions or 1 large onion, halved and thickly sliced

2 celery ribs/sticks, chopped into 1-cm/½-in. pieces

2 carrots, peeled, sliced into quarters lengthways and chopped into 1-cm/½-in. pieces

750 g/1 lb. 10 oz. organic minced/ ground beef

10 chestnut mushrooms, halved

400 g/14 oz. passata/strained tomatoes

1 tablespoon tamari or coconut aminos

½ teaspoon salt

2 tablespoons tomato paste

1 tablespoon dried oregano

Serves 6

# BEEF BOLOGNESE

*Beef bolognese can also be made as a sauce in the multi-cooker. If you prefer to cook the pasta separately or serve the bolognese over a vegetable-based pasta alternative, this is the vegetable- filled, flavour-packed bolognese sauce recipe you need.*

Press the Sauté button on the multi-cooker and add the oil. When hot, add the onions, celery and carrots and stir until the onions become translucent. Next, add the beef and stir to break up any lumps. Once the beef has browned, add the mushrooms, passata/strained tomatoes, tamari or coconut aminos, salt, tomato paste and oregano. Stir to combine and deglaze the pot (see page 4).

Secure the lid in place and set to Manual or High Pressure for 15 minutes. At the end of cooking, use the NPR method (see page 4). Serve immediately.

# PANCETTA AND TOMATO PASTA

1 tablespoon ghee or butter
1 onion, chopped
200 g/7 oz. diced pancetta
   or bacon
2 garlic cloves, crushed
1 tablespoon coconut aminos
   or tamari
1 courgette/zucchini, chopped
500 ml/2 cups vegetable stock
400 g/14 oz. passata/strained
   tomatoes
320 g/11 oz. brown rice fusilli
grated Parmesan, to serve

Serves 4

*This is a really quick and easy meal made
from straightforward ingredients.*

Press the Sauté button on the multi-cooker and add the ghee or
butter. When melted, add the onion and pancetta or bacon. Stir for
about 3 minutes, then add the garlic and stir for another 2 minutes.
Add the coconut aminos or tamari and deglaze the pot (see page 4),
then add all the remaining ingredients and stir.

   Secure the lid in place and set to Manual or High Pressure for
2 or 3 minutes (the pasta cooking time is reduced to one-third of
the time stated on the package). At the end of cooking, use the QPR
method (see page 4), open the lid and stir. Then leave the pasta in
the pot until the desired consistency is reached. Serve sprinkled
with grated Parmesan.

# PEA AND PAPRIKA CREAMY PASTA

25 g/$\frac{1}{2}$ cup nutritional
   yeast flakes
1$\frac{1}{2}$ teaspoons salt
$\frac{1}{2}$ teaspoon onion powder
$\frac{1}{2}$ teaspoon garlic powder
$\frac{1}{2}$ teaspoon smoked paprika
3 tablespoons olive oil
1 tablespoon freshly squeezed
   lemon juice
1 large sweet potato
   (about 400 g/14 oz.),
   peeled and cubed
4 medium tomatoes,
   chopped into wedges
250 g/9 oz. pea pasta
grated/shredded vegan cheese
   or sliced avocado, to serve

Serves 3

*This pasta dish is 'creamy' and luxurious in taste.
It's a delicious and nutritious vegan pasta dish.*

In a bowl, mix together the nutritional yeast flakes, salt, onion
powder, garlic powder and paprika. In a separate bowl mix together
the olive oil and lemon juice.

   Put the sweet potato cubes and tomato wedges into the
multi-cooker. Add the nutritional yeast mixture and the olive oil
mixture and stir. Add the pea pasta and 650 ml/2$\frac{3}{4}$ cups water,
then push all the pasta down into the water.

   Secure the lid in place and set to Manual or High Pressure
for 2 minutes. At the end of cooking, use the QPR method
(see page 4). Serve with a sprinkling of vegan cheese or
some sliced avocado.

# BUTTERNUT SQUASH, CHORIZO AND ONION ON COURGETTI

1½ tablespoons olive oil

2 onions, cut into wedges

150 g/5½ oz. chorizo, thickly sliced

½ large butternut squash, peeled, deseeded and cut into large cubes

35 ml/2½ tablespoons coconut aminos or tamari

4 courgettes/zucchinis, made into courgetti using a spiralizer or julienne peeler (or a shop-bought bag of courgetti, available in most supermarkets)

Serves 2

*For health reasons or allergy reasons, many people like to switch out wheat-based pasta for vegetable alternatives. This courgetti is a great addition to the combined flavours of chorizo and butternut squash and makes for a lower-carb but nutrient-rich meal for two.*

Press the Sauté button on the multi-cooker and add the olive oil. When hot, add the onions to the pot and stir until nearly translucent. Add the chorizo and butternut squash and stir again. Add the coconut aminos or tamari and 2½ tablespoons water and stir again to deglaze the pot (see page 4).

Secure the lid in place and set to Manual or High Pressure for 3 minutes. At the end of cooking, use the QPR method (see page 4). Add the courgetti and stir to combine, then replace the lid and leave to 'mellow' for 2 minutes before serving.

# SAUSAGE AND TOMATO SAUCE WITH COURGETTI

1 teaspoon olive oil

6 sausages, skins removed

1 tub of fresh pasta sauce (preferably tomato and basil)

4 courgettes/zucchinis, made into courgetti using a spiralizer or julienne peeler (or a shop-bought bag of courgetti, available in most supermarkets)

Serves 2

*A ridiculously simple four-ingredient recipe, ideal for busy midweek evenings.*

Press the Sauté button on the multi-cooker and add the olive oil, then crumble in the sausage meat. Break down the sausage meat with a wooden spoon until it resembles minced/ground meat in texture. Add the pasta sauce and stir.

Secure the lid in place and set to Manual or High Pressure for 4 minutes. At the end of cooking, use the QPR method (see page 4), then stir in the courgetti and let soften for a couple of minutes.

# CHEESE-FILLED MEATBALLS IN A CHUNKY TOMATO SAUCE

## FOR THE MEATBALLS
½ onion, very finely chopped
1 garlic clove, crushed
1 tablespoon barbecue sauce
   (ideally one with no added
   sugar)
1 tablespoon tomato paste
1 teaspoon Dijon mustard
1 teaspoon salt
800 g/1 lb. 12 oz. minced/
   ground beef
1 large egg or 1 duck egg
50 g/1 cup fresh breadcrumbs,
   gluten-free breadcrumbs
   or rice crumbs
100 g/1 cup finely grated
   Cheddar cheese

## FOR THE SAUCE
1 teaspoon olive oil
½ onion, chopped
1 garlic clove, crushed
2 celery stalks, chopped
1 teaspoon salt
1 tablespoon balsamic vinegar
1 tablespoon tomato paste
1 x 400-g/14-oz. can
   chopped tomatoes
1 teaspoon dried oregano

Serves 4

*These meatballs are what my children describe as 'comfort food'. Good served with spaghetti.*

First, make the meatballs. Mix together the onion, garlic, barbecue sauce, tomato paste, mustard, salt, beef, egg and bread- or rice crumbs. Roll into about 15–17 balls, then flatten each one into a flat patty. Place a small mound of grated/shredded cheese in the centre of each, then close the meat up around the cheese to enclose it in a meatball.

To make the sauce, press the Sauté button on the multi-cooker and add the olive oil. When hot, add the onion, garlic and celery. Stir for a couple of minutes, then add the salt, vinegar and tomato paste and keep stirring for another few minutes. Next, add the tomatoes and deglaze the pan (see page 4), then stir in the oregano.

Place the meatballs in the sauce. Secure the lid in place and set to Manual or High Pressure for 20 minutes. At the end of cooking, use the NPR method (see page 4).

**Note:** if you prefer a smoother sauce, once cooked, remove the meatballs and process the sauce to a much smoother consistency before serving alongside/over the meatballs.

## APRICOT TURKEY MEATBALLS

*Light, fruity and flavoursome turkey meatballs.*

1 x 400-g/14-oz. can apricot
   halves in natural juice, drained
30 g/1 oz. spring onions/scallions
   (white part only – use the green
   part as a garnish), very finely
   chopped
2 garlic cloves, crushed
¼ teaspoon ground mace
¼ teaspoon ground cinnamon
500 g/1 lb. 2 oz. minced/
   ground turkey
½ teaspoon salt
30 g/⅓ cup ground almonds
40 ml/2½ tablespoons tamari
   or coconut aminos
½ teaspoon finely chopped
   fresh ginger
⅛ teaspoon ground nutmeg

Serves 4

Place the apricot halves in a food processor and process to a purée. Remove from the food processor and set aside. Put the spring onions/scallions, garlic, mace, cinnamon, turkey, salt and ground almonds in the food processor and process to combine. Roll the mixture into 12 equally-sized meatballs.

In the multi-cooker, mix 60 g/4 tablespoons apricot purée with the tamari or coconut aminos, ginger and nutmeg. Add the meatballs.

Secure the lid in place and set to Manual or High Pressure for 10 minutes. At the end of cooking, use the NPR method (see page 4).

To thicken the sauce, remove the meatballs and wrap in foil to keep warm. Press the Sauté button on the multi-cooker and stir the sauce until thickened. Serve the meatballs and sauce together, garnished with the chopped green spring onions/scallions.

## MEATBALLS WITH LENTIL PASTA

*These meatballs are moist and succulent thanks to the added vegetables. The lentil pasta makes this a very substantial dish for a family.*

800 g/1 lb. 12 oz. minced/
   ground beef
2 eggs
½ courgette/zucchini,
   finely diced
1 carrot, finely diced
1½ teaspoons salt
1 teaspoon dried oregano
50 g/4 tablespoons ground
   flaxseeds/linseeds
1 x 400-g/14-oz. can chopped
   tomatoes
2 tablespoons barbecue sauce
   (ideally one without added
   sugar)
1 tablespoon coconut aminos
   or tamari
1 vegetable stock cube or
   1 tablespoon vegetable
   stock paste (see page 31)
250 g/9 oz. lentil pasta

Makes 20-22 meatballs/
Serves 6

In a bowl, mix together the beef, eggs, courgette/zucchini, carrot, salt, oregano and flaxseeds/linseeds. Form into meatballs about the size of large golf balls (this can get a little messy so I wear catering gloves).

Put the tomatoes, barbecue sauce, coconut aminos or tamari, stock cube or paste and 400 ml/1⅔ cups water into the multi-cooker. Add the meatballs and push them under the sauce.

Secure the lid in place and set the Meat button for 12 minutes. At the end of cooking, use the NPR method (see page 4). Remove the meatballs and cover to keep warm.

Add the pasta to the pot. Secure the lid and cook on Manual or High Pressure for 2 minutes. At the end of cooking, use the QPR method (see page 4) and serve the pasta and meatballs together.

# RICE AND GRAINS

# COURGETTE, FETA AND MINT RISOTTO

2 tablespoons olive oil

2 small courgettes/zucchinis, chopped

1/4 teaspoon salt

2 onions, chopped

2 garlic cloves, crushed

75 ml/5 tablespoons dry white wine

250 g/2 1/4 cups Arborio rice

2 tablespoons vegetable stock paste (see page 31) or 2 vegetable stock cubes

150-g/5 1/2-oz. feta cheese, cubed

10 g/1/3 cup finely chopped fresh mint

Serves 6

*This dish was created for a retreat I worked on in Corfu many years ago. A Sunday Times journalist on that particular trip raved about it and asked for the recipe, which she shared on her own travel blog. Including the recipe in this book was a no-brainer as the multi-cooker lends itself so well to risottos.*

Press the Sauté button on the multi-cooker and add the oil. When hot, sauté the courgettes/zucchinis, sprinkling the salt over during sautéing. Remove to a bowl when coloured and soft. Add the onions to the pot. Cook for a few minutes, then add the garlic and wine and deglaze the pot (see page 4). Next, add the rice, stock paste/cubes and 600 ml/2 1/2 cups water and stir.

Secure the lid in place and set to Manual or High Pressure for 6 minutes. At the end of cooking, use the QPR method (see page 4) and stir in the cooked courgettes/zucchinis, feta and chopped mint. Good served with a green salad.

# CASHEW NUT PILAFF

2 tablespoons olive oil or avocado oil

1 onion, very finely chopped or grated

1 garlic clove, crushed

1 carrot, grated

250 g/1 1/2 cups basmati rice, rinsed

1 teaspoon salt

1 teaspoon ground cumin

1 teaspoon ground coriander

1/2 teaspoon ground turmeric

100 g/3/4 cup roasted cashew nuts

2 tablespoons freshly chopped coriander/cilantro

Serves 4

*Cashews lend a really sweet flavour and nutty texture to this pilaff. Make sure you add the fresh coriander/cilantro as this herb really makes this dish.*

Press the Sauté button on the multi-cooker and add the oil. When hot, add the onion, garlic and carrot. Stir for about 5 minutes. Add the rice, salt and spices and stir well. Add 320 ml/1 1/3 cups water and deglaze the pan (see page 4).

Secure the lid in place and set to Rice for 12 minutes. At the end of cooking, use the QPR method (see page 4). Immediately stir in the cashew nuts and chopped coriander/cilantro and serve.

# MUSHROOM RISOTTO

1 tablespoon olive oil

1 large onion, finely chopped

3 garlic cloves, finely chopped

250 g/1⅓ cups Arborio rice

1 chicken or vegetable stock cube
or 1 tablespoon vegetable stock
paste (see page 31)

75 ml/5 tablespoons dry white
wine, at room temperature

1 teaspoon salt

1 teaspoon dried thyme

200–250 g/7–9 oz. mixed
mushrooms (including some
Asian varieties), chopped into
small pieces

freshly squeezed juice of
½ lemon

3 handfuls fresh spinach

55 g/½ cup grated/shredded
mature Cheddar cheese

salt and freshly ground
black pepper

Serves 4

*A creamy mushroom risotto made
using classic ingredients.*

Press the Sauté button on the multi-cooker and add the oil.
When hot, sauté the onion and garlic for 3 minutes.

Add the rice and stir well. Add the stock cube or vegetable
paste, 600 ml/2½ cups water, the wine, salt, thyme and
mushrooms and stir once again to ensure the ingredients are
thoroughly mixed.

Secure the lid in place and set to Manual or High Pressure for
6 minutes. At the end of cooking, use the QPR method (see page 4)
to prevent the risotto from overcooking. Stir in the lemon juice,
spinach, grated/shredded cheese and salt and pepper to taste.
Stir well. If it's still a little too liquid, just let it sit for a couple of
minutes as it will thicken as it cools. Serve with a mixed salad.

# CHICKEN AND BACON RISOTTO

1 tablespoon olive oil

1 onion, finely chopped

2 garlic cloves, crushed

4 slices of bacon, chopped

10 mushrooms, thickly sliced

500 g/1 lb. 2 oz. chicken,
cut into cubes

150 ml/⅔ cup white wine

300 g/1⅔ cups Arborio rice

1 vegetable stock cube or
1 tablespoon vegetable stock
paste (see page 31)

1 tablespoon freshly chopped
thyme

1 tablespoon butter

grated pecorino or Parmesan
cheese, to serve

freshly ground black pepper

Serves 4

*A very comforting meal achieved with minimal effort.
The multi-cooker means there is no need to stand over
the hob stirring constantly to create the perfect risotto.*

Press the Sauté button on the multi-cooker and add the oil.
When hot, add the onion, garlic, bacon, mushrooms and chicken
and sauté for about 3 minutes. Add the wine to the pot to deglaze
(see page 4). After a couple more minutes, stir in the rice, stock cube
or paste, thyme and 600 ml/2½ cups water and stir really well.

Secure the lid in place and set to Rice for 12 minutes.
At the end of cooking, use the QPR method (see page 4). Stir the
risotto well to develop the creamy texture, then stir in the butter.
Leave to stand for 3 minutes, then serve topped with Parmesan
and freshly ground black pepper.

# SPANISH RICE WITH MINCED PORK

75 g/1 cup finely grated
  Parmesan cheese
60 g/2 oz. chorizo, finely chopped
1 onion, ½ grated and ½ chopped
500 g/1 lb. 2 oz. minced/
  ground pork
1 tablespoon ghee
1 plump garlic clove, thinly sliced
2 carrots, chopped
1 tablespoon vegetable stock
  paste (see page 31) or
  1 vegetable stock cube
1 teaspoon paprika
250 g/1½ cups basmati rice,
  rinsed
shavings of Manchego or
  Parmesan cheese, to serve

Serves 4

*This family favourite combines the salty flavours of
Parmesan and chorizo with mellow minced/ground
pork and rice in a delicious meal.*

In a food processor or by hand, mix the Parmesan, chorizo, grated
onion and minced/ground pork.

Press the Sauté button on the multi-cooker and add the ghee.
When hot, fry the chopped onion, garlic and carrots for 5 minutes,
then add the pork mixture and stir, using a spoon to break up the
mixture, until the pork is coloured. Add the stock paste or cube
and stir, then add the paprika, rice and 320 ml/1⅓ cups water
and deglaze the pan (see page 4).

Secure the lid in place and set to Rice for 12 minutes. At the end
of cooking, use the QPR method (see page 4) and serve immediately
with shavings of Manchego or Parmesan cheese on the top.

# BUTTERNUT SQUASH
# AND CHORIZO GOLDEN RICE

310 g/11 oz. butternut squash,
  peeled, deseeded and cubed
115 g/4 oz. chorizo, cubed
250 g/1½ cups basamati rice,
  rinsed
2 tablespoons butter or ghee
salt and freshly ground
  black pepper

Serves 6 as a side dish

*A deliciously buttery rice side dish
that's a beautiful golden colour.*

Place the butternut squash, chorizo, rice and 320 ml/11 fl. oz.
water in the multi-cooker.

Secure the lid in place and set to Rice for 12 minutes. At the
end of cooking, use the QPR method (see page 4) and open the lid.
Stir in the butter or ghee and the seasoning, then serve.

# SPEEDY VEGETABLE BIRYANI

2 tablespoons butter, ghee, avocado oil or olive oil

1 onion, coarsely grated

1 carrot, coarsely grated

1 courgette/zucchini, coarsely grated

2 garlic cloves, finely grated

10 mushrooms, thickly sliced

250 g/1½ cups basmati rice, rinsed

1 teaspoon salt

¾ teaspoon ground cumin

½ teaspoon ground turmeric

Serves 4

*This is our family's favourite rice dish. It can be enjoyed alone, with other Indian veggie dishes or even eaten cold as part of a buffet or packed lunch the next day.*

Press the Sauté button on the multi-cooker and add the butter, ghee or oil. When melted or hot, add the onion, carrot, courgette/zucchini, garlic and mushrooms. Stir for about 5 minutes. Add the rice, salt and spices and stir well. Add 320 ml/1⅓ cups water and deglaze the pan (see page 4).

Secure the lid in place and set to Rice for 12 minutes. At the end of cooking, use the QPR method (see page 4), then serve.

# PEA AND CORN RICE

2 tablespoons olive oil

1 large onion, chopped

¼ teaspoon salt

2 tablespoons freshly chopped coriander/cilantro

2 garlic cloves, crushed

1 teaspoon ground turmeric

125 g/4½ oz. canned or frozen sweetcorn/corn kernels

150 g/1¼ cups frozen peas

250 g/1½ cups basmati rice, rinsed

1 tablespoon vegetable stock paste (see page 31) or 1 vegetable stock cube

2 tablespoons butter or ghee, or olive oil for a vegan dish

Serves 4 as a side dish

*This is one of the simplest rice dishes but it's a great dish for those who love peas and corn. In my work as a nutritionist I've met so many people who tell me these are their favourite two vegetables. Pea and sweetcorn lovers, this dish is for you!*

Press the Sauté button on the multi-cooker and add the olive oil. When hot, add the onion and sprinkle with the salt. Cook for about 5 minutes, stirring regularly. Add the coriander/cilantro, garlic and turmeric and stir again, then add the sweetcorn, peas and rice. Stir once again, then add 320 ml/1⅓ cups water and the stock paste or cube, then deglaze the pan (see page 4).

Secure the lid in place and set to Rice for 12 minutes. At the end of cooking, use the QPR method (see page 4). Stir in the butter, ghee or oil and serve.

# MEDITERRANEAN CHICKEN WITH RICE

1 tablespoon ghee

1 onion, chopped

2 garlic cloves, crushed

2 teaspoons smoked paprika

¾ teaspoon salt

4 tomatoes, quartered

2 chicken breasts, sliced

approx. 20 French/green beans, topped, tailed and chopped into 1-cm/½-in. lengths

250 g/1½ cups basmati rice, rinsed

1 chicken stock cube or 1 tablespoon vegetable stock paste (see page 31)

24 pitted/stoned black olives

1 pot of marinated artichokes

4 slices of Parma ham or prosciutto, torn roughly

Serves 4

*This is a very simple chicken and rice dish. It's a great meal to put together if you have unexpected guests for dinner.*

Press the Sauté button on the multi-cooker and add the ghee. When melted, add the onion and garlic and stir constantly for about 4 minutes. Then add the paprika, salt, tomatoes, chicken and French/green beans and stir. Stir in the rice, then add 320 ml/11 fl. oz. water and the stock cube or paste.

Secure the lid in place and set to Rice for 12 minutes. At the end of cooking, use the QPR method (see page 4). Stir in the olives, artichokes and torn Parma ham or prosciutto. Serve immediately.

# QUINOA PILAFF

1 tablespoon butter or
   avocado oil
1 onion, chopped
½ green chilli/chile, chopped
3 carrots, finely chopped
1 teaspoon freshly grated ginger
3 garlic cloves, crushed
140 g/5 oz. frozen spinach
85 g/¾ cup frozen peas
170 g/1 cup quinoa
1 teaspoon salt

Serves 4

*Quinoa is known as a pseudo-grain. It's actually closely related to beetroot/beet and spinach. It provides a nutrient-dense base ingredient for this pilaff.*

Press the Sauté button on the multi-cooker and add the butter or oil. When hot, add the onion, chilli/chile, carrots, ginger and garlic and stir until the onion is almost transparent. Add the spinach and peas and stir once more. Then add the quinoa, salt and 230 ml/1 cup water, giving the pot a final stir.

    Secure the lid in place and set to Manual or High Pressure for 2 minutes. At the end of cooking, use the NPR method (see page 4).

# MUSHROOM QUIN-OTTO

2 tablespoons avocado oil,
   olive oil or butter
1 onion, finely chopped
20 g/¾ oz. dried shiitake
   mushrooms or mixed dried
   mushrooms, soaked in water
   for as long as it says on the
   packaging (reserve the
   soaking water)
3 garlic cloves, crushed
170 g/1 cup quinoa, rinsed
½ teaspoon salt
½ teaspoon freshly ground
   black pepper
1 teaspoon dried thyme
2 tablespoons grated Parmesan,
   pecorino or vegan cheese

Serves 4 as a main meal
with a side salad

*This is like a mushroom risotto but made using quinoa rather than rice. Use oil and vegan cheese to make this purely vegan.*

Press the Sauté button on the multi-cooker and add the oil or butter. When hot, add the onion and cook for 5 minutes. Add the mushrooms, garlic, quinoa, salt, pepper and thyme plus 250 ml/1 cup of the mushroom soaking water and stir to deglaze the pot (see page 4).

    Secure the lid in place and set to Manual or High Pressure for 2 minutes. At the end of cooking, use the QPR method (see page 4) and stir the cheese into the quin-otto before you serve.

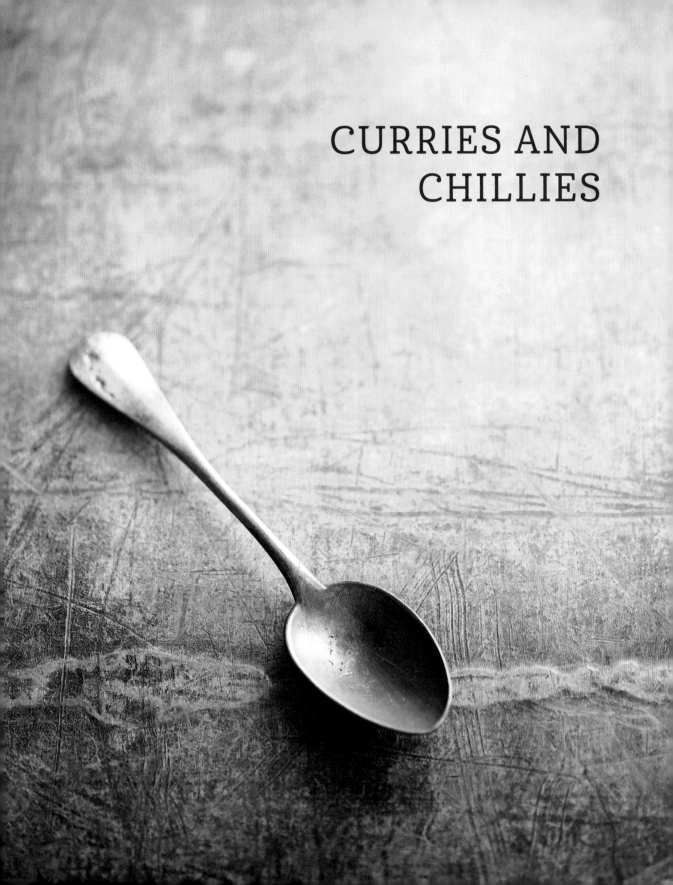

# CURRIES AND CHILLIES

# CHICKEN TIKKA MASALA

2 onions, chopped
1 garlic clove, crushed
1-cm/¹/₂-in. piece of fresh
   ginger, grated
2 teaspoons garam masala
³/₄ teaspoon paprika
³/₄ teaspoon ground turmeric
1 teaspoon ground cumin
¹/₂ teaspoon ground cinnamon
2 teaspoons salt
500-g/18-oz. can passata/
   strained tomatoes
450 g/1 lb. boneless chicken
   breasts, cut into bite-sized
   pieces
¹/₂ x 400-g/14-oz. can coconut
   milk (ideally the thick, creamy
   part of it which has separated)

Serves 4

*No take-out curry order would be complete without ordering this dish, yet it can be made in minutes in your own home using very straightforward ingredients.*

Put all the ingredients except the coconut milk into the multi-cooker, making sure the chicken goes in last so it doesn't stick to the bottom during cooking.

Secure the lid in place and set to Poultry for 15 minutes. At the end of cooking, use the QPR method (see page 4). Add the coconut milk, stir and keep warm in the pot until ready to serve. Serve the curry on Cauliflower Rice (see page 85) or basmati rice.

# ALMOND SATAY

50 g/2 oz. chopped peeled
   sweet potato
75 g/2³/₄ oz. French/green beans
2 boneless chicken breasts, sliced
   into mini fillets
5 drops of fish sauce
1 teaspoon freshly grated ginger
1 teaspoon tamari or coconut
   aminos
80 g/5¹/₂ tablespoons almond
   butter
200 ml/³/₄ cup coconut milk

Serves 2

*This is a rich and 'creamy' dairy-free dish. Satay is, of course, traditionally made using peanut butter or ground peanuts, but as almonds are more nutritious and simply delicious, I've used them instead.*

Place the vegetables and chicken pieces in the multi-cooker. In a bowl, mix together the fish sauce, grated ginger, tamari or coconut aminos, almond butter and coconut milk. (If the almond butter is fridge-hard, you may need to soften it a little by mixing with a drop of warm water before adding it to the sauce.) Pour the sauce into the pot and stir to mix.

Secure the lid in place and set to Manual or High Pressure for 3 minutes. At the end of cooking, use the NPR method (see page 4).

# BEEF MASSAMAN WITH NEW POTATOES

1 tablespoon ghee

2 onions, sliced

2 carrots, chopped

500 g/1 lb. 2 oz. minced/
  ground beef

2 tablespoons massaman
  curry paste

1½ teaspoons tamari or coconut
  aminos

¼ teaspoon fish sauce

100 ml/6 tablespoons coconut
  milk

350 g/12 oz. new potatoes,
  cut in half

freshly chopped coriander/
  cilantro, to garnish

Serves 3–4

*This is a simply delicious, all-in-one mid-week meal. This Thai-style curry is mild and full of authentic flavour.*

Press the Sauté button on the multi-cooker and add the ghee. When melted, add the onions and carrots and sauté for a few minutes. Add the beef and break it up to allow even browning. Add the curry paste, tamari or coconut aminos, fish sauce and coconut milk, then stir to deglaze the pot (see page 4).

Secure the lid in place and set to Manual or High Pressure for 10 minutes. At the end of cooking use the QPR method (see page 4).

Add the potatoes to the pot. Secure the lid in place and set to Manual or High Pressure for 4 minutes. At the end of cooking, use the NPR method (see page 4). Garnish with coriander/cilantro.

# RED THAI BEEF CURRY

1 tablespoon ghee

2 onions, each sliced into 8 wedges

2 garlic cloves, thinly sliced

900 g/2 lb. casserole/stewing
  beef, cubed

1 tablespoon Thai red curry paste
  (ideally one without added sugar)

1 teaspoon fish sauce

1 teaspoon salt

1 teaspoon coconut sugar

1 teaspoon balsamic vinegar

1 teaspoon tamari or coconut
  aminos

200 ml/¾ cup thick coconut milk

2 sweet potatoes, peeled, halved
  and chopped into large chunks

300 g/10½ oz. fresh spinach

4 tablespoons coconut yogurt
  or soured/sour cream, to serve

freshly chopped coriander/
  cilantro, to garnish

Serves 6

*What's not to love about a Thai curry? This one has a vibrant and appealing colour and, with only a small amount of spice, won't deter spice-detecting palates.*

Press the Sauté button on the multi-cooker and add the ghee. When melted, add the onions and garlic and cook, stirring with a wooden spoon, for about 5 minutes. Next, add the beef and stir to ensure the outside of most pieces is browned. Add the curry paste, fish sauce, salt, coconut sugar, balsamic vinegar and tamari or coconut aminos and deglaze the pot (see page 4). Add the coconut milk and sweet potatoes and give one more stir.

Secure the lid in place and set to Manual or High Pressure for 25 minutes. At the end of cooking, use the NPR method (see page 4). Open the lid and add in the spinach, stirring until all the leaves have wilted. Serve with coconut yogurt or soured/sour cream on top and a scattering of freshly chopped coriander/cilantro.

# AROMATIC PANEER CURRY

1 onion, chopped

3 tomatoes, cut into quarters

5 baby aubergines/eggplants,
cut into quarters (or 1 large
aubergine/eggplant chopped
into 2 x 2-cm/³/₄ x ³/₄-in. pieces)

1 green chilli/chile, finely chopped

1 teaspoon freshly grated ginger

2 tablespoons ghee

2 sprigs of fresh curry leaves
(optional)

1 tablespoon freshly chopped
coriander/cilantro

¹/₂ teaspoon date syrup or
maple syrup

¹/₂ teaspoon salt

4 teaspoons korma paste

2 teaspoons avocado oil or
olive oil

500 g/1 lb. 2 oz. paneer, cubed

Serves 4

*Paneer cheese has a delicious texture – it's a little bit like
halloumi but softer. It makes for a great vegetarian curry.*

Place the onion, tomatoes, aubergines/eggplants, chilli/chile,
ginger, ghee, curry leaves, coriander/cilantro, date or maple syrup,
salt and 80 ml/5¹/₂ tablespoons water in the multi-cooker. Secure
the lid in place and set to Manual or High Pressure for 10 minutes.

Meanwhile, mix the korma paste and oil together in a large
bowl and tip in the paneer cubes. Toss the paneer with your hands
or a spoon to coat.

When the curry sauce is cooked, use the QPR method (see
page 4). Remove the curry leaves. Using a stick blender or food
processor, blend the contents of the inner pot. Press the Sauté
button and allow the sauce to bubble for 5 minutes, then add the
korma-coated paneer. Cook for a further 5 minutes, then serve.

# VEGETABLE CURRY

1 tablespoon ghee, butter
or avocado oil

1 onion, chopped

1 teaspoon freshly grated ginger

1 small green chilli/chile, finely
chopped

2 carrots, chopped

1 teaspoon ground cumin

¹/₂ teaspoon ground turmeric

¹/₄ teaspoon chilli/chili powder

1 heaped teaspoon salt

1 small cauliflower, chopped
into large florets

2 tomatoes, cut into eighths

160 ml/²/₃ cup canned coconut
cream

Serves 4

*A simple veggie curry – simple ingredients
and simple to make.*

Press the Sauté button on the multi-cooker and add the ghee,
butter or oil. When hot, add the onion, ginger, chilli/chile and
carrots. Stir until the onion is just becoming translucent. Add the
spices and salt and stir well, then stir in the cauliflower florets and
tomatoes. Add the coconut cream and give everything one last stir
to deglaze the pan (see page 4).

Secure the lid in place and set to Manual or High Pressure for
2 minutes. At the end of cooking, use the QPR method (see page 4)
and serve.

# SAAG (INDIAN SPINACH)

**1 tablespoon ghee or avocado oil**
**1 onion, chopped**
**2 garlic cloves, crushed**
**2.5 x 5-cm/1 x 2-in. piece of fresh**
   **ginger, peeled and grated**
**¾ teaspoon salt**
**½ teaspoon ground coriander**
**¼ teaspoon ground turmeric**
**½ teaspoon ground cumin**
**½ teaspoon mustard powder**
**500 g/1 lb. 2 oz. frozen spinach**
   **(in cubes)**

Serves 4 as a side dish

*A delightfully aromatic Indian side dish. It's a great accompaniment to many of the rice dishes in this book.*

Press the Sauté button on the multi-cooker and add the ghee or oil. When hot, add the onion. Stir until translucent, then add the garlic and ginger and stir briefly, then add all the remaining ingredients and 3 tablespoons water.

Secure the lid in place and set to Manual or High Pressure for 4 minutes. At the end of cooking, use the QPR method (see page 4). Open the pot and stir, then serve with naan or hot dosa.

# SAG ALOO (SPINACH AND POTATO CURRY)

**2 tablespoons butter, ghee,**
   **avocado oil or olive oil**
**1 onion, chopped**
**560 g/1 lb. 4 oz. potatoes,**
   **peeled and chopped**
**½ red chilli/chile, deseeded**
   **and chopped**
**300 g/10½ oz. frozen spinach**
**2 garlic cloves, sliced**
**1 tablespoon freshly grated**
   **ginger**
**1 teaspoon salt**
**½ teaspoon ground turmeric**
**½ teaspoon ground cumin**
**½ teaspoon nigella/black**
   **onion seeds**

Serves 4 as a side dish

*A curry take-away favourite for many, this spinach and potato dish can work as a standalone curry but it's even better served alongside another vegetable curry.*

Press the Sauté button on the multi-cooker and add the butter, ghee or oil. When hot, add the onion, potatoes, chilli/chile and spinach. Stir for about 5 minutes, then add the garlic, ginger, salt and spices and 200 ml/¾ cup water and stir to deglaze the pan (see page 4).

Secure the lid in place and set to Manual or High Pressure for 3 minutes. At the end of cooking, use the QPR method (see page 4), then serve.

## THAI CHICKEN WITH CAULIFLOWER RICE

1 tablespoon butter

1 teaspoon olive oil

1 large cauliflower, chopped into florets, then processed to a 'rice' consistency in a food processor (alternatively, buy a supermarket packet of prepared cauliflower 'rice')

2 garlic cloves, crushed

2 sweet potatoes, peeled and chopped

25 French/green beans, topped and tailed (fresh or frozen)

1½ teaspoons Thai blend of dry spices

2 tablespoons tamari or coconut aminos

1 teaspoon fish sauce

1 teaspoon freshly grated ginger

1 x 400-ml/14-fl. oz. can coconut milk

4 boneless chicken breasts, sliced

Serves 4

*An aromatic Thai curry served with low-carbohydrate cauliflower rice.*

Press the Sauté button on the multi-cooker and add the butter and oil. When hot, add the cauliflower rice and stir constantly for about 5 minutes until the rice is just coloured. Remove from the pot, place in a warm bowl and cover with foil to keep warm.

Add all the remaining ingredients to the pot. Secure the lid in place and set to Manual or High Pressure for 3 minutes. At the end of cooking, use the QPR method (see page 4). Serve over the cauliflower rice.

## MALAYSIAN CHICKEN

1 teaspoon ghee

2 onions, roughly chopped

1 large garlic clove, chopped

6 boneless chicken breasts

2 teaspoons Malaysian spice mix

1½ tablespoons tamari or coconut aminos

1½ teaspoons fish sauce

300 ml/1¼ cups canned coconut milk

15–20 mangetout/snow peas

Serves 6

*Malaysian flavours are subtle and aromatic in this easy-to-make curry dish.*

Press the Sauté button on the multi-cooker and add the ghee. When hot, add the onions and sauté for 5 minutes, then add the garlic and chicken. Seal the chicken all over, then add the spice, tamari or coconut aminos, fish sauce and coconut milk and deglaze the pot (see page 4).

Secure the lid in place and set to Manual or High Pressure for 12 minutes. At the end of cooking, use the NPR method (see page 4). Open the lid and stir in the mangetout/snow peas. Allow to cook in the residual heat for up to 5 minutes, then serve. Delicious over roasted turmeric cauliflower or with butternut squash 'spaghetti'.

1 onion

3 celery stalks

10 g/4 tablespoons freshly
chopped coriander/cilantro

180 g/6½ oz. butternut squash

1 tablespoon olive oil

3 tablespoons tomato paste

1 teaspoon garlic powder

1½ tablespoons mild curry
powder

160 g/1 cup split red lentils,
washed thoroughly

1 tablespoon vegetable
stock paste (see page 31)
or 1 vegetable stock cube

freshly squeezed lemon juice
(up to ½ lemon)

salt and freshly ground black
pepper

Serves 4

# MILD BUTTERNUT DHAL

*Partnering sweet butternut squash with the dense texture of
cooked lentils really makes this dhal stand out. The addition
of lemon juice makes it sparkle even more.*

Very finely chop the onion, celery, coriander/cilantro and butternut
squash. (Using a food processor at this stage will save you a lot
of time.)

Press the Sauté button on the multi-cooker and add the olive oil.
When hot, add the finely chopped vegetables to the pot and stir until
the onion becomes translucent. Add the tomato paste, garlic powder
and curry powder and stir well. Add the lentils, stock paste or cube
and 750 ml/3 cups water and deglaze the pan (see page 4).

Secure the lid in place and set to Manual or High Pressure for
3 minutes. At the end of cooking, use the NPR method (see page 4)
for 15 minutes, then release the rest of the pressure using the QPR
method. Serve with added lemon juice and salt and pepper to taste.

1 tablespoon olive oil or avocado oil

1 teaspoon cumin seeds

1 onion, chopped

2 garlic cloves, finely chopped

1 tablespoon finely chopped
fresh ginger

1 small chilli/chile, finely chopped
(omit this if serving to children
who don't like the heat)

1 teaspoon garam masala

¾ teaspoon ground coriander

½ teaspoon ground turmeric

1 teaspoon salt

170 g/1 cup quinoa

135 g/5 oz. passata/strained
tomatoes

1 x 400-g/14-oz. can chickpeas,
drained

lime pickle, to serve

Serves 3

# CHANA MASALA QUINOA

*Chickpeas feature widely in Asian cuisine. They absorb flavour
so well, as in this dish of chickpeas and quinoa combined with
Asian spices. A pickle served with the dish works wonderfully.*

Press the Sauté button on the multi-cooker and add the oil. When
hot, add the cumin seeds and stir until fragrant, then add the onion
and stir. Next add the garlic and ginger and stir, then add the other
spices, salt and quinoa. Add the passata and 125 ml/8 tablespoons
water to the pot. Deglaze the pan (see page 4).

Secure the lid in place and set to Manual or High Pressure
for 2 minutes. At the end of cooking, use the QPR method
(see page 4). Stir in the chickpeas and leave to warm
through, then serve with lime pickle.

# LAMB SAAG

1 teaspoon cumin seeds

1 teaspoon coriander seeds

1 onion

2-cm/¾-in. piece of fresh ginger

2 plump garlic cloves, peeled

2 tablespoons freshly chopped
   coriander/cilantro

1 tablespoon ghee

450 g/1 lb. boneless lamb, cubed

4 tomatoes, quartered

2 cardamom pods

¾ teaspoon ground turmeric

1 teaspoon salt

230 g/4 cups baby spinach
   leaves, rinsed

Serves 2–3

*This is delicious served with Speedy
Vegetable Biryani (see page 68).*

Press the Sauté button on the multi-cooker.
Put the cumin and coriander seeds in the pot.
Once you start to smell the aroma from the
seeds, transfer them to a food processor. Add
the onion, ginger, garlic and coriander/cilantro
and chop finely.

Add the ghee to the pot. When melted, add
the contents of the food processor. Stir for about
3 minutes, then add the lamb and brown on all
sides. Add the tomatoes, cardamom, turmeric
and salt and stir. Add 125 ml/8 tablespoons
water and stir.

Secure the lid in place and set to Meat/Stew
for 35 minutes. At the end of cooking, use the
NPR method (see page 4). Stir in the spinach
before serving.

## GREEN BEAN AND CAULIFLOWER CURRY

90 g/3¼ oz. frozen French/
    green beans
500 g/1 lb. 2 oz. cauliflower,
    cut into large florets
1 onion, finely chopped
2 tomatoes, chopped
2 carrots, chopped
150 ml/⅔ cup coconut milk
1 teaspoon salt
1 teaspoon vegetable stock paste
    (see page 31)
1½ teaspoons medium curry
    powder
1 teaspoon freshly grated ginger
freshly chopped coriander/
    cilantro, to garnish

Serves 4

*This is a very simple curry recipe that's great for using
up vegetables. It's very quick to make, too, so one for those
evenings when you are too tired to think.*

Put all the vegetables in the multi-cooker. In a bowl, mix together
the coconut milk, salt, stock paste, curry powder and ginger.
Add this mixture to the pot and stir.

Secure the lid in place and set to Manual or High Pressure for
1 minute. At the end of cooking, use the QPR method (see page 4).
Serve with coriander/cilantro sprinkled over the top.

## AUBERGINE AND CAULIFLOWER CURRY

1 teaspoon yellow mustard seeds
2 tablespoons avocado oil
    or olive oil
2 onions, chopped
2 garlic cloves, crushed or grated
1 teaspoon freshly grated ginger
2 medium aubergines/eggplants,
    chopped into 3 x 3-cm/
    1¼ x 1¼-in. pieces
1 large cauliflower, chopped into
    large florets
1 x 400-g/14-oz. can crushed
    tomatoes
1 teaspoon salt
1 x 400-g/14-oz. can chickpeas,
    drained and rinsed
2 tablespoons curry powder
natural/plain yogurt and freshly
    chopped coriander/cilantro,
    to serve

Serves 4

*This is an option for a busy weekday evening as it uses mostly
storecupboard ingredients and doesn't need much planning.
It goes well with Speedy Vegetable Biriyani (see page 68).*

Press the Sauté button on the multi-cooker. Add the mustard seeds
and dry-fry until they darken in colour. Remove from the pot and
discard. Add the oil to the pot and when hot, add the onions, garlic
and ginger, stirring until the onions start to soften. Add
the aubergines/eggplants and cauliflower and stir. Add
the crushed tomatoes, salt, chickpeas, curry powder
and 110 ml/½ cup water and deglaze the pot
(see page 4).

Secure the lid in place and set to Manual
or High Pressure for 3 minutes. At the end
of cooking, use the NPR method (see
page 4). Serve with a dollop of
plain yogurt and a sprinkling
of fresh coriander/cilantro.

## AUBERGINE AND WHITE SWEET POTATO BHAJI CURRY

3 tablespoons olive oil, avocado oil, butter or ghee
1 onion, chopped
6 baby aubergines/eggplants, cut into quarters
2 white sweet potatoes, peeled and chopped
2 garlic cloves, grated
3-cm/1¼-in. piece of fresh ginger, grated
1 teaspoon salt
1 teaspoon garam masala
1 teaspoon ground cumin
6 cherry tomatoes, halved

Serves 4

*Soft, succulent aubergines/eggplants combine with the mellow flavour of white sweet potato in this delicious veggie curry.*

Press the Sauté button on the multi-cooker and add the oil, butter or ghee. Once hot or melted, add the onion, aubergines/eggplants and sweet potatoes. Stir for about 7 minutes, then add the garlic and ginger with the salt and spices and stir again. Finally, add the cherry tomatoes and 70 ml/5 tablespoons water and deglaze the pan (see page 4).

Secure the lid in place and set to Manual or High Pressure for 2 minutes. At the end of cooking, use the QPR method (see page 4).

## MILD CHILLI BEEF WITH SWEET POTATO AND BLACK BEANS

1 tablespoon olive oil
2 onions, chopped
500 g/1 lb. 2 oz. minced/ground beef
½ teaspoon cumin seeds
¼ teaspoon mild chilli/chili powder
½ teaspoon ground coriander
½ teaspoon smoked paprika
2 garlic cloves, chopped
3 tablespoons tomato paste
1 stock cube or 1 tablespoon vegetable stock paste (see page 31)
1 large sweet potato, peeled and chopped
1 x 400-g/14-oz. can chopped tomatoes
1 x 400-g/14-oz. can black beans, drained and rinsed
soured/sour cream and guacamole, to serve

Serves 4

*This is a mild chilli ideal for anyone sensitive to spice and heat. Kidney beans are replaced by black beans as they have a slightly sweeter taste, which may appeal to younger diners.*

Press the Sauté button on the multi-cooker and add the oil. When hot, add the onions and stir for 4 minutes. Add the beef, cumin seeds, chilli/chili powder, coriander and paprika and stir again, ensuring the bottom of the pan is deglazed (see page 4). Once the beef is brown, add the garlic, tomato paste and stock cube or paste and 140 ml/⅔ cup water and deglaze again. Add the sweet potato and canned tomatoes.

Secure the lid in place and set to Manual or High Pressure for 15 minutes. At the end of cooking, use the QPR method (see page 4), then press Sauté, add the black beans and stir. Serve the after 5 minutes, with a dollop of sour/soured cream and guacamole on top.

## CHILLI BEEF AND MUSHROOMS

1 tablespoon ghee

1 large onion, sliced

3 garlic cloves, chopped

500 g/1 lb. 2 oz. minced/
 ground beef

1 tablespoon balsamic vinegar

1 tablespoon tamari or coconut
 aminos

1 teaspoon coconut sugar

2 teaspoons chilli/chili powder

1 teaspoon ground cumin

1/4 teaspoon ground cinnamon

3 allspice berries

3 tablespoons tomato paste

200 g/7 oz. button mushrooms,
 cleaned but left whole

sliced avocado and soured/
 sour cream, to serve

Serves 4

*This dish is all about umami, our fifth taste. It's packed full of flavour and texture, from the melt-in-the-mouth mushrooms to the strong flavours of balsamic vinegar, tamari and coconut.*

Press the Sauté button on the multi-cooker and add the ghee. When hot, add the onion and garlic and stir. After 3 minutes, add the beef and break it up with a wooden spoon. Once browned, add the balsamic vinegar, tamari or coconut aminos, sugar, chilli/chili powder, cumin, cinnamon, allspice berries and tomato paste and stir to deglaze the pot (see page 4). Finally, stir in the mushrooms.

Secure the lid in place and set to Manual or High Pressure for 10 minutes. At the end of cooking, use the NPR method (see page 4). Serve in deep bowls with sliced avocado and soured/sour cream.

## SPICY MINCED PORK

1 1/2 teaspoons olive oil

1 onion, chopped

2 carrots, diced into 1 x 1-cm/
 1/2 x 1/2-in. pieces

1 courgette/zucchini, diced into
 2 x 2-cm/3/4 x 3/4-in. pieces

1 garlic clove, finely chopped

500 g/1 lb. 2 oz. minced/
 ground pork

1 tablespoon tomato paste

1 teaspoon smoked paprika

1 teaspoon coconut sugar

3/4 teaspoon salt

200 g/7 oz. canned cherry
 tomatoes

150 g/5 1/2 oz. mushrooms,
 cut into quarters

1 teaspoon dried oregano

sliced avocado and soured/
 sour cream, to serve

Serves 4

*Pork, paprika and tomato are simply made for one another. These delicious flavours combine in this sumptuous spicy pork dish.*

Press the Sauté button on the multi-cooker and add the oil. When hot, add the onion, carrots and courgette/zucchini and sauté until the onion is translucent. Add the garlic and pork and stir, breaking up the meat with a spoon, until the pork has browned. Add the tomato paste, paprika, coconut sugar, salt and tomatoes and stir again, being sure to deglaze the pot (see page 4). Add the mushrooms and oregano and give the mix one last stir.

Secure the lid in place and set to Manual or High Pressure for 15 minutes. At the end of cooking, use the NPR method (see page 4). Serve with sliced avocado and a dollop of soured/sour cream on top.

# CASSEROLES
# AND ROASTS

# LAMB RACK STEW

3½ tablespoons red wine
1 tablespoon tomato paste
1 tablespoon barbecue sauce
   (ideally one with no added
   sugar)
1 teaspoon smoked paprika
1 tablespoon tamari or coconut
   aminos
½ teaspoon garlic powder
a pinch of dried rosemary
1 teaspoon salt
4 celery stalks, cut into
   5-cm/2-in. lengths
4 carrots, cut into
   3-cm/1¼-in. lengths
3 tomatoes, cut into quarters
650 g/1 lb. 7 oz. rack of lamb,
   cut in half

Serves 2

*This stew is characterized by the
tenderness of the lamb, which is literally
falling off the bone when it is served. This
stew is so comforting and full of delicious
ingredients that just work so well together.*

Place all the ingredients apart from the lamb rack
in the multi-cooker, add 150 ml/⅔ cup water and
stir. Add the lamb rack.

Secure the lid in place and set to Manual
or High Pressure for 30 minutes. At the end of
cooking, use the NPR method (see page 4) and
then serve.

# LAMB TAGINE

¾ teaspoon ground cinnamon
¾ teaspoon ground turmeric
¾ teaspoon ground ginger
1 teaspoon ground cumin
1 teaspoon salt
2 tablespoons date nectar
    or honey
2 tablespoons olive oil, plus
    1 tablespoon for cooking
800 g/1 lb. 12 oz. lamb shoulder,
    diced
1 onion, chopped
2 garlic cloves, sliced
6 organic dried apricots, sliced
2 sweet potatoes, peeled and
    chopped
a handful of toasted flaked/
    slivered almond

Serves 6

*This dish has the taste and smell of a souk in Marrakesh.
It's so aromatic, yet uses everyday spices.*

In a small bowl or ramekin, make a paste from the spices, salt, date nectar or honey and 2 tablespoons of the olive oil. Place the diced lamb in a large bowl, add the spice paste and stir to coat the lamb.

Press the Sauté button on the multi-cooker and add the remaining 1 tablespoon olive oil. When hot, add the onion and garlic and stir rapidly for 4 minutes, then add the paste-coated lamb and keep stirring. After another 3 minutes, add the apricots and sweet potatoes.

Secure the lid in place and set to Stew for 20 minutes. At the end of cooking, use the NPR method (see page 4). Serve each bowlful with some toasted flaked/slivered almond scattered over the top. This tagine is good served with couscous.

# MOROCCAN LAMB

1 tablespoon avocado oil or ghee
400 g/14 oz. soffrito (a mix of
    carrot, celery and onion,
    chopped and ready to cook)
3 tablespoons harissa paste
2 teaspoons salt
2 tablespoons tomato paste
800 g/1 lb. 12 oz. minced/
    ground lamb
2 sweet potatoes, peeled
    and chopped
sliced avocado, to serve

Serves 4

*This is one of those meals you'll be extremely grateful
for during busy times. It takes very little time to prepare,
especially if you buy a pack of ready-chopped vegetables,
and the result tastes fabulous.*

Put everything apart from the sliced avocado into the multi-cooker and stir. Secure the lid in place and set to Manual or High Pressure for 18 minutes. At the end of cooking, use the NPR method (see page 4). Serve in bowls with sliced avocado on top.

# SEAFOOD STEW

500 g/1 lb. 2 oz. skinless
   halibut or cod fillets,
   cut into bite-sized pieces
1 teaspoon freshly squeezed
   lime juice
1 tablespoon ghee or butter
1 onion, chopped
1 garlic clove, crushed
1 courgette/zucchini,
   thickly sliced
1 x 200-g/7-oz. can chopped
   tomatoes
250 ml/1 cup coconut milk
1 teaspoon salt
250 g/9 oz. raw king prawns/
   shrimp, peeled
freshly chopped parsley,
   to garnish
lemon wedges, to serve

Serves 4

*Fish dishes are often some of the tastiest
due to the sauce the fish is served in. The
multi-cooker can make great-tasting
sauces in a short period of time, and fish
that needs very little cooking can be added
at the end of pressure cooking so it is just
soft and flaking when you eat the dish.*

Place the fish in a shallow dish and squeeze
or drizzle over the lime juice, then toss the fish
with your hands to coat each piece. Set aside.

Press the Sauté button on the multi-cooker
and add the ghee or butter. When melted, add the
onion and stir for about 5 minutes. Add the garlic,
courgette/zucchini, chopped tomatoes, coconut
milk and salt.

Secure the lid in place and set to Manual
or High Pressure for 5 minutes. At the end of
cooking, use the QPR method (see page 4). Add
the fish and the prawns/shrimp to the dish and
stir. Set the multi-cooker to Keep Warm until they
are just cooked. Serve immediately, garnished
with parsley and with lemon wedges on the side.

# CHICKEN CACCIATORE

1 tablespoon olive oil
1 onion, roughly chopped
2 celery stalks, roughly chopped
4 slices of bacon, cut into thin
    strips
1 garlic clove, chopped
400 g/14 oz. mini chicken fillets
1 teaspoon coconut sugar
1 teaspoon salt
1 tablespoon tomato paste
1 teaspoon dried rosemary
6 mushrooms, cut into quarters
1 x 400-g/14-oz. can chopped
    tomatoes
20 pitted/stoned black olives

Serves 4

*Succulent chicken fillets combine with salty bacon and fruity tomatoes in this delicious Italian classic.*

Press the Sauté button on the multi-cooker and add the oil. When hot, add the onion and celery and stir for 3 minutes, then add the bacon and garlic and stir for another 2 minutes. Add the chicken and stir for another 3 minutes. Add the coconut sugar, salt, tomato paste, rosemary, mushrooms, tomatoes and black olives.

Secure the lid in place and set to Manual or High Pressure for 7 minutes. At the end of cooking, use the NPR method (see page 4) and serve immediately.

# CAJUN CHICKEN AND PEPPER CASSEROLE

1 tablespoon ghee
1/2 green (bell) pepper,
    1/2 red (bell) pepper and
    1/2 yellow/orange (bell) pepper,
    all deseeded and sliced
    3-cm/1¼-in. thick
2 onions, halved and sliced
8 chicken thighs, skin on and
    bone in
2 garlic cloves, crushed
1 tablespoon smoked paprika
1 teaspoon onion powder
1 teaspoon mustard powder
2 teaspoons salt
2 teaspoons coconut sugar
1/2 teaspoon dried marjoram
    or oregano
1/2 teaspoon dried thyme
1 tablespoon red wine vinegar
250 g/9 oz. passata/strained
    tomatoes

Serves 4

*A great combination of flavours – Cajun spices with peppers and chicken. This is sure to be a crowd-pleaser.*

Press the Sauté button on the multi-cooker and add the ghee. When hot, add half the (bell) peppers, all the onions and all the chicken thighs. Sauté until the onions are translucent. Remember to deglaze the pan (see page 4) with a splash of water to make sure the base of the pan has no bits stuck to the bottom.

Meanwhile, create a Cajun paste – mix the garlic, paprika, onion powder, mustard powder, salt, sugar, herbs and red wine vinegar in a small bowl. Add this to the pot and stir. Finally, add the passata/strained tomatoes and stir again.

Secure the lid in place and set to Poultry for 15 minutes. At the end of cooking, use the NPR method (see page 4). Stir in the remaining (bell) peppers and leave to mellow for a couple of minutes before serving. Great served over Cauliflower Rice (see page 85).

# BEEF AND PAPRIKA STEW

1 tablespoon ghee or butter

1 onion, chopped

450 g/1 lb. casserole/stewing beef, roughly chopped

1 courgette/zucchini, chopped into 3-cm/1¼-in. lengths

3 sweet potatoes, peeled and chopped into 3 x 3-cm/ 1¼ x 1¼-in. pieces

2 large carrots, chopped into 3-cm/1¼-in. lengths

2 teaspoons sea salt

1 teaspoon mixed herbs

1½ teaspoons smoked paprika, plus extra to serve

1 teaspoon garlic powder

1 teaspoon onion powder

2 tablespoons tomato paste or beetroot/beet ketchup

1½ teaspoons Worcestershire sauce (gluten-free if preferred)

soured/sour cream, to serve

Serves 4

*Inspired by a recipe given to me by a Hungarian friend, this stew is full of flavour and the meat is simply melt-in-the-mouth gorgeous.*

Press the Sauté button on the multi-cooker and add the ghee or butter. When melted, add the onion and stewing beef. Sauté until the beef is no longer pink, then add the courgette/zucchini, sweet potatoes and carrots. Stir to combine, then add all the seasonings and stir once more.

Secure the lid in place and set to Stew for 30 minutes. Make sure the steam valve is closed. At the end of cooking, use the NPR method (see page 4). Serve with a generous dollop of soured/sour cream on top and a sprinkling of smoked paprika.

# MUM'S BEEF STEW

1 teaspoon olive oil

1 large onion, chopped

2 garlic cloves, sliced

2 celery stalks, thickly sliced

4 carrots, thickly sliced

3 potatoes, unpeeled, chopped to same size pieces as the carrots

800 g/1 lb. 12 oz. casserole/ stewing beef, cubed

200 ml/¾ cup red wine

1 tablespoon date nectar or honey

1 tablespoon tomato paste

1 teaspoon dried mixed herbs

1 teaspoon salt

1 teaspoon smoked paprika

Serves 4

*This is a firm favourite in our family. The combination of smoky paprika and sweet honey combines with the beef and veggies to create a really hearty stew.*

Press the Sauté button on the multi-cooker and add the oil. When hot, add all the vegetables and the beef. Stir for about 7 minutes. Don't worry if not all the beef is coloured.

Meanwhile, mix together the red wine, date nectar or honey, tomato paste and herbs. Add the salt and paprika to the pot and stir, then add the red wine mix and deglaze the pan (see page 4).

Secure the lid in place and set to Stew for 35 minutes. At the end of cooking, use the NPR method (see page 4) for 20 minutes, then use the QPR method and serve.

# CAJUN PULLED CHICKEN

2 tablespoons vegetable stock
    paste (see page 31)
500 g/1 lb. 2 oz. boneless
    chicken breasts, sliced into
    100-g/3½-oz. pieces
½ teaspoon Cajun spice mix

HONEY AND MUSTARD DRESSING
110 g/½ cup mayonnaise
60 ml/4 tablespoons extra virgin
    olive oil
2 tablespoons red wine vinegar
2 tablespoons raw honey
2 tablespoons Dijon mustard
1 tablespoon chopped onion
½ teaspoon sea salt

Serves 4

*A combination of flavours and textures that is sure to please. This succulent and beautifully spiced pulled chicken is ideal served with a mixed salad.*

To make the dressing, place all the ingredients in a blender and blend thoroughly. Set aside.

    Mix the stock paste with 100 ml/⅓ cup water in the multi-cooker. Add the chicken pieces and sprinkle over the Cajun spice.

    Secure the lid in place and set to Poultry for 10 minutes. At the end of cooking, use the NPR method (see page 4). Open the lid once the pressure has released. Shred the chicken using a couple of forks or a blunt knife and a fork – it should break away easily. Serve with a mixed salad and a drizzle of the honey and mustard dressing.

# SMOKY BARBECUE CHICKEN

2–3 chicken breasts
6–7 carrots, cut into
    3-cm/1¼-in. lengths

MARINADE
50 g/2 oz. passata/strained
    tomatoes
2½ teaspoons tomato purée
3 tablespoons molasses or
    black treacle
1 tablespoon maple syrup
¾ tablespoon apple cider vinegar
2 teaspoons salt
1½ teaspoons smoked paprika
    (or slightly less if you don't like
    too much heat)
1 teaspoon wholegrain mustard
½ teaspoon garlic powder

Serves 2–3

*The appealing flavour of this dish comes from the addition of molasses or black treacle and paprika.*

In a large container, mix together the marinade ingredients, then place the chicken breasts in the marinade. Place in the fridge and leave to marinate for at least 30 minutes, but ideally for a couple of hours.

    When you are ready to cook, place everything into the multi-cooker. Secure the lid in place and set to Manual or High Pressure for 10 minutes. At the end of cooking, leave for 5 minutes, then use the QPR method (see page 4), then serve.

# WHOLE ROAST LEMON CHICKEN

1 teaspoon smoked paprika
1 teaspoon dried thyme
1/2 teaspoon garlic salt
3/4 teaspoon salt
1/4 teaspoon ground black pepper
1 x 1.8-kg/4-lb. chicken
1/2 lemon
1 tablespoon ghee or coconut oil
300 ml/1¼ cups chicken stock
    (if using a stock cube, omit
    the salt from the seasoning)
3 tablespoons red wine
3 large potatoes, peeled and
    cut into quarters

Serves 4

*This is such an impressive way to serve up an evening meal. Roast chicken no longer has to be reserved for Sundays when you can make one this simply and quickly in the pot.*

In a small bowl or ramekin, mix together the smoked paprika, dried thyme, garlic powder, salt, and pepper. Rub the dry seasoning over the skin of the chicken. Put the lemon half inside the chicken cavity.

Press the Sauté button on the multi-cooker and add the ghee or coconut oil. When hot, push the chicken down into the pot. Try to sear all surfaces of the chicken by moving it around and pushing it down onto the base of the pot. Once seared on all surfaces, take the chicken out carefully and rest on a plate.

Add the stock and red wine to the pot, ensuring you deglaze the pot with a wooden spoon (see page 4). Add the potatoes to the pot and rest the trivet on top, being careful not to burn yourself on the hot inner pot. Place the chicken on the trivet.

Secure the lid in place and set to Manual or High Pressure for 30 minutes. At the end of cooking, use the NPR method (see page 4).

To serve, place the chicken and potatoes on a serving plate, and serve the sauce separately in a small jug/pitcher.

# LEG OF LAMB IN RED WINE JUS

1 tablespoon butter

1.5–2-kg/3¼–4½-lb. leg
   of lamb, bone in

2 onions, chopped

250 ml/1 cup red wine

1 tablespoon vegetable stock
   paste (see page 31)
   or 1 vegetable stock cube

4 large potatoes, peeled and
   chopped into thirds

10 carrots, left whole

Serves 6–8

*In the early days of our marriage, my husband and I would rely on a particular 7-hour lamb recipe whenever we had guests. We knew it was a reliable and impressive recipe, so we just made sure we never served it to the same guests twice. We then tweaked it a little when the kids came along, to suit our collective tastes. So when I saw that Mike Vrobel from dadcooksdinner.com had recreated the original version in the multi-cooker, I cooked our version in the pot using his recommended cooking times. It works like a dream!*

Press the Sauté button on the multi-cooker and add the butter. When melted, add the lamb and sear on all sides. This will take about 5 minutes. Remove the lamb to a plate.

Add the onions to the pot. If they start to stick a little, use some of the red wine to deglaze the pan (see page 4). Add the rest of the red wine and when it starts to evaporate, add 250 ml/1 cup water, the stock paste or cube, potatoes and carrots. Place the lamb joint on top.

Secure the lid in place and set to Manual or High Pressure for 90 minutes. At the end of cooking, use the NPR method (see page 4). Serve the lamb with the vegetables and some of the jus.

# PORK BELLY WITH WHITE CABBAGE

35 ml/2 tablespoons tamari or
   coconut aminos
1 tablespoon honey
1 teaspoon freshly grated ginger
1/8 teaspoon ground allspice
2 garlic cloves, crushed
5 drops of brown rice vinegar
600 g/1 lb. 5 oz. pork belly,
   thickly sliced
1/2 white cabbage, sliced into
   thick wedges

Serves 4

*A very easy dish that is cost-effective and a real palate pleaser.*

In a medium bowl, combine the tamari or coconut aminos, honey, ginger, allspice, garlic and vinegar with 3½ tablespoons water.

Press the Sauté button on the multi-cooker. When up to heat, add the pork belly and immediately pour over the tamari/ coconut aminos mix. Deglaze the pot (see page 4) with a spoon as you move the pork slices around the pot. Once the pork slices are seared on all sides, add the cabbage wedges.

Secure the lid in place and set to Manual or High Pressure for 30 minutes. At the end of cooking, use the NPR method (see page 4). Serve with jacket sweet potatoes (see page 126).

# WHOLE GAMMON

200 ml/3/4 cup (hard) cider
3 very large potatoes, peeled
   and cut into thirds lengthways
   (omit if making ham only)
4 whole carrots, trimmed
   (omit if making ham only)
1 teaspoon salt
   (omit if making ham only)
1 x unsmoked gammon joint

Serves 4-6

*This is a great way to cook gammon as a family meal or to make ham for multiple family meals throughout the week. This method is actually the one chosen by a wonderful friend and Instant Pot® expert Maria Bravo. She recommends cooking your gammon for 11 minutes per 1 lb. (that's just under 450 g) and that's what works for me. So whatever your size of gammon you can use this method and simply adjust the time.*

Place the cider and 100 ml/⅓ cup water in the multi-cooker. Add the vegetables to the pot, then the salt. Place the gammon joint on top of the vegetables.

Secure the lid in place and set to Manual or High Pressure for 11 minutes per 500 g/1 lb. 2 oz. of gammon. At the end of cooking, use the NPR method (see page 4). Serve the gammon sliced with the vegetables and some of the cooking liquid from the base of the pot.

# COTTAGE PIE

1 tablespoon ghee or butter
1 onion, chopped
500 g/1 lb. 2 oz. minced/
    ground beef
2 carrots, chopped
1 celery stalk, chopped
1 tablespoon tomato ketchup
    (ideally a low-sugar version)
1 tablespoon tamari or coconut
    aminos
1 tablespoon barbecue sauce
    (ideally a low-sugar version)
1 tablespoon vegetable
    stock paste (see page 31)
    or 1 vegetable stock cube
300-g/10½-oz. canned chopped
    tomatoes
4 medium potatoes, peeled
    and cut into quarters
2 tablespoons butter
1 tablespoon almond milk
1 tablespoon arrowroot
2 tablespoons grated/shredded
    mature Cheddar, pecorino
    or vegan cheese

Serves 4

*This is a lovely 'pot in pot' pie. That means the potatoes can cook at the same time as the sauce, but without being in the sauce.*

Press the Sauté button on the multi-cooker and add the ghee or butter. When melted, add the onion and sauté for 5 minutes, then add the beef and stir until browned, breaking it up as you go. Add the carrots, celery, ketchup, tamari or coconut aminos, barbecue sauce, stock paste or cube and tomatoes, plus 100 ml/⅓ cup water and stir.

Line the steamer basket with foil and place the potatoes and 190 ml/¾ cup water in the steamer basket. Place the trivet (ideally a long-legged one) in the pot and place the steamer basket on top.

Secure the lid and set to Meat for 15 minutes. At the end of cooking, use the NPR method (see page 4).

Drain the potatoes, transfer to a bowl and mash them with the butter and almond milk until smooth. Cover the bowl with foil to keep the mashed potato warm.

Using a slotted spoon, spoon or transfer the meat mixture into the base of an oven dish. Cover with foil to keep warm. Take 4 tablespoons of the liquid in the pot and stir with the arrowroot. Add this back into the pot and press the Sauté button – the sauce will thicken after 5–6 minutes. Add this sauce to the meat, then spoon the mashed potato on top and sprinkle over the cheese. Pop under a preheated grill/broiler until the cheese is melted.

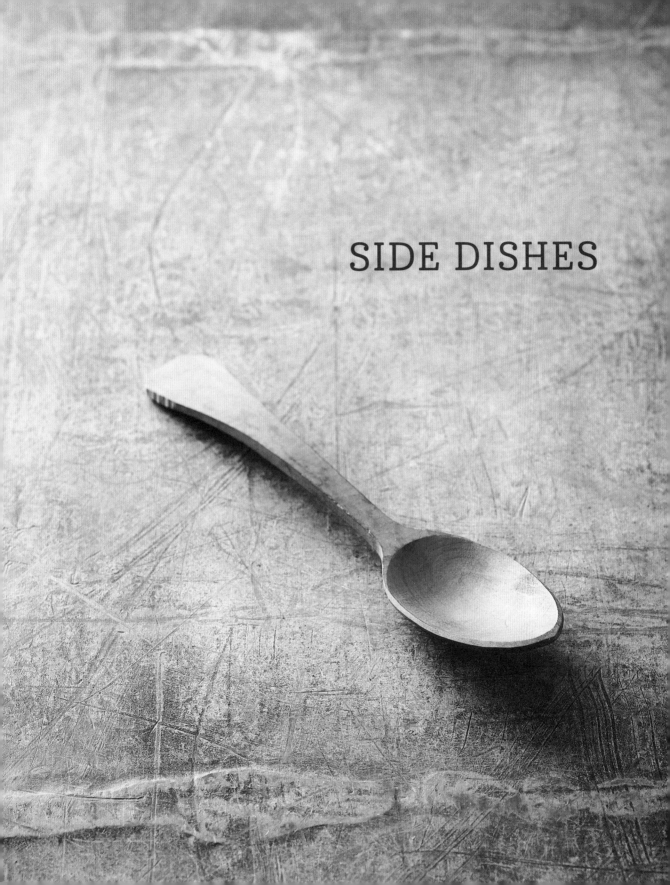

SIDE DISHES

# BRUSSELS SPROUTS WITH BACON AND CHESTNUTS

1 tablespoon butter

4 slices of streaky bacon, chopped

20 Brussels sprouts, trimmed and scored on the bottom

1 tablespoon tamari or coconut aminos

120 g/4¼ oz. whole cooked chestnuts, peeled (you can buy these ready roasted in the supermarket)

Serves 4 as a side dish

*I always jazz up Brussels sprouts – I think this stems from the early days of parenthood when I wasn't convinced the children would eat them without bells and whistles!*

Press the Sauté button on the multi-cooker and add the butter. When melted, sauté the bacon until cooked, then add the Brussels sprouts, tamari or coconut aminos and 2 tablespoons water.

Secure the lid in place and set to Manual or High Pressure for 3 minutes. At the end of cooking, use the QPR method (see page 4). Add the chestnuts to the pan and stir until warmed through.

# CAULIFLOWER MASH

1 cauliflower (about 500 g/ 1 lb. 2 oz. once leaves and most of stem removed)

1 teaspoon salt

1 teaspoon ground cumin

½ teaspoon coconut sugar

40 g/3 tablespoons salted butter or vegan spread

Serves 4 as a side dish

*This dish provides the comfort of mashed potato but is much lower in carbohydrates and more nutritious. You may wonder why the cauliflower is cooked whole in this recipe. One reason is that it saves a lot of time, the other is that it avoids making a mess while chopping up the cauliflower at the start of cooking. Pressure cooking a whole cauliflower is so quick that you don't need to chop it up first to create deliciously creamy mash.*

Carefully remove most of the cauliflower stem, but leave enough in place so that the florets stay intact. Place the cauliflower on the trivet in the multi-cooker. Add 250 ml/1 cup water to the pot. Sprinkle over the salt, cumin and coconut sugar.

Secure the lid in place and set to Manual or High Pressure for 10 minutes. At the end of cooking use the QPR method (see page 4).

Remove the cauliflower from the pot and place in a food processor (you may need to break it up a little to fit it in) with the butter or vegan spread. Process to a 'mashed potato' consistency, then serve.

# BBQ BAKED BEANS

250 g/9 oz. dried haricot/navy
    beans, soaked overnight in a
    bowl with water to cover (yields
    500 g/1 lb. 2 oz. once soaked)
1½ teaspoons salt
1 tablespoon molasses
1½ teaspoons maple syrup
½ teaspoon ground allspice
¼ teaspoon garlic powder
¼ teaspoon onion powder
50 g/3 tablespoons tomato
    purée/paste
300 g/10½ oz. passata/
    strained tomatoes
grated/shredded vegan or
    Cheddar cheese, to serve
    (optional)

Serves 4

*Baked beans have become a British institution, yet they
originated with Native Americans. This recipe is more
authentic and closer to the original recipes than modern
canned beans. While Native Americans used animal fat
in their recipe, I've made this a vegan version.*

Drain and rinse the soaked beans, then place them in the multi-
cooker with all the other ingredients (except the cheese) and
150 ml/⅔ cup water.

Secure the lid in place and set to Manual or High Pressure for
25 minutes. At the end of cooking, use the NPR method (see page 4).
Serve on slices of buttered sourdough toast or Grain-free Bread
(see page 19). If you wish, scatter some grated cheese over the top.

# JERK BAKED BEANS

1 tablespoon olive oil
1 onion, chopped
3 slices of streaky bacon,
    chopped into small pieces
2 x 400-g/14-oz. cans white
    beans (cannellini or haricot/
    navy beans work well),
    drained and rinsed
500 g/1 lb. 2 oz. passata/
    strained tomatoes
1 tablespoon honey
½ teaspoon treacle
½ teaspoon jerk seasoning
¼ teaspoon smoked paprika
⅛ teaspoon ground allspice
¾ teaspoon salt

Serves 8

*This slightly spicy version of the classic
baked beans makes a really delicious change.*

Press the Sauté button on the multi-cooker and add the oil. When
hot, add the onion and bacon and stir for about 5 minutes. Add all
the other ingredients and stir to deglaze the pan (see page 4).

Secure the lid in place and set to Manual or High Pressure for
2 minutes. At the end of cooking, use the NPR method (see page 4).
These beans taste delicious served on buttered sourdough toast
or Grain-free Bread (see page 19).

# RED CABBAGE

600 g/1 lb. 5 oz. red cabbage,
   shredded using a mandolin
   or sharp knife
2 eating apples, cored and grated
2 onions, chopped
1/4 teaspoon freshly grated
   nutmeg
1/4 teaspoon ground cloves
1/4 teaspoon ground cinnamon
1 tablespoon coconut sugar
1 teaspoon vegetable stock paste
   (see page 31) or 1/3 vegetable
   stock cube
3 tablespoons red wine vinegar
2 tablespoons butter or
   coconut oil
freshly ground black pepper

Serves 4–6 as a side dish

*Spicy and sweet red cabbage complements
many of the heartier dishes in this book.*

Put the cabbage, apples and onions in the multi-cooker and
sprinkle/drizzle over the spices, sugar, stock paste or cube
and vinegar, plus 100 ml/1/3 cup water, then dot with the butter
or coconut oil.

   Secure the lid in place and set to Manual or High Pressure
for 3 minutes. At the end of cooking, use the QPR method
(see page 4), then serve.

# GREEN CABBAGE, BACON AND LEEKS

25 g/1 3/4 tablespoons butter
4 slices of streaky bacon,
   chopped into small pieces
250 g/9 oz. thinly sliced leeks
   and sliced green cabbage,
   mixed together

Serves 4 as a side dish

*This is a very quick and simple side dish. It is a great
way to use up that last leek and the half a cabbage left
over from Sunday lunch.*

Press the Sauté button on the multi-cooker and add the butter.
When melted, add the bacon and sauté until coloured. Add
the vegetables and 1 tablespoon water and deglaze the pot
(see page 4).

   Secure the lid in place and set to Manual or High Pressure
for 3 minutes. At the end of cooking, use the QPR method
(see page 4), then serve.

# CORN ON THE COB

**3 corn on the cob/ears of corn, broken in half if you wish**
**3 tablespoons butter**
**freshly ground black pepper**

Serves 3–6

*This is simply the sweetest, quickest, tastiest way to prepare corn on the cob.*

Pour 300 ml/1¼ cups water into the multi-cooker. Place the corn in the steaming basket on the trivet inside the pot.

Secure the lid in place and set to Manual or High Pressure for 3 minutes. At the end of cooking, use the QPR method (see page 4). Eat straight away, dotted with butter and black pepper.

# 'BAKED' JACKET SWEET POTATOES

**3 x 230-g/8-oz. sweet potatoes, skins scrubbed in water using a potato brush or scouring cloth**
**3 teaspoons butter or soured/ sour cream**

Serves 3

*No peeling. No fuss. No mess. This way of preparing sweet potatoes is hassle-free. The results are deliciously soft 'baked' sweet potatoes. These are tasty served with butter or soured/sour cream.*

Place 250 ml/1 cup water in the base of the multi-cooker. Insert the metal trivet and place the potatoes on their sides on the trivet in a single layer.

Secure the lid in place and set to Manual or High Pressure for 20 minutes. At the end of cooking, use the QPR method (see page 4). Serve with a teaspoon of butter or soured/sour cream on each potato.

# SWEET THINGS

# 'BAKED' APPLES WITH NUTTY FILLING

3 Bramley apples
60 g/4 tablespoons salted butter,
   at room temperature
60 g/4 tablespoons maple syrup
80 g/³/₄ cup mixed chopped
   nuts (or chopped nuts of
   your choice)
½ teaspoon ground cinnamon
¼ teaspoon ground ginger
¼ teaspoon ground allspice

Serves 3

*Cooking apples in the multi-cooker is a really quick way to create a tasty dessert. They're moist and full of flavour.*

Remove the core from the apples. In a bowl, mix together the butter, maple syrup, nuts and spices. Cut three large squares of foil and place an apple upright on each. Fill the cored hole with the nut mixture. Wrap the apples in the foil.

Place 250 ml/1 cup water in the multi-cooker. Place the trivet in the pot and the foil-wrapped apples on top of the trivet.

Secure the lid in place and set to Manual or High Pressure for 10–15 minutes, depending on the size of the apples (very large apples will need the full 15 minutes). At the end of cooking, use the QPR method (see page 4), then serve.

# SEEDED APPLE CRUMBLE

3 eating apples, peeled and cored
100 g/1 cup gluten-free rolled/
   old-fashioned oats
50 g/¹/₃ cup mixed seeds
25 g/2 tablespoons coconut sugar
½ teaspoon ground cinnamon
75 g/¹/₃ cup salted butter
Greek yogurt, to serve

Serves 6

*A deliciously comforting dish using the natural sweetness of apples to create a tasty base, and with seeds mixed with the crumble to give texture and a great flavour to the topping.*

Chop the apples into wedges. Lay these in the base of a flat-bottomed, round heatproof glass dish.

In a separate bowl, mix together the oats, seeds, sugar and cinnamon, then add the butter and rub together with your fingertips. Spoon the crumble over the top of the layered apple.

Pour 300 ml/1¹/₄ cups water into the multi-cooker. Add the trivet and place the crumble dish on top.

Secure the lid in place and set to Manual or High Pressure for 10 minutes. At the end of cooking, use the NPR method (see page 4). Serve warm or cold with Greek yogurt.

# BUTTERNUT AND CINNAMON CHEESECAKE

**BASE**
**160 g/5½ oz. gluten-free oatcakes**
**20 g/1½ tablespoons coconut sugar**
**80 g/5½ tablespoons butter, melted**

**TOPPING**
**2 tablespoons coconut flour**
**1 teaspoon ground cinnamon, plus extra for dusting**
**a pinch of salt**
**150 g/5½ oz. puréed steamed butternut squash**
**250 g/1¼ cups cream cheese**
**60 g/5 tablespoons coconut sugar**
**3 eggs**

15-cm/6-in. diameter deep, round springform cake pan

Serves 8

*This recipe is inspired by Julia Levy-Twomey who posted a version of this cheesecake on a social media group. Her opening gambit was 'I'm Jewish and I have New York in my veins...' before outlining how to pressure-cook the perfect cheesecake. That's the sort of commendation that sparks intrigue on my part and all I can say is that I am so glad she posted the original version, because this cheesecake is dreamy. My version is gluten-free, too.*

Line the base of the cake pan with baking parchment.

For the base, in a food processor, grind the oatcakes and sugar to a powder, then add the melted butter and process again. Push this into the base of the cake pan, using the back of a cold spoon to achieve an even spread.

Put all the topping ingredients into your food processor and combine. Pour into the cake pan over the base. Wrap one sheet of foil over the pan, covering the top fully so the folds of foil are under the pan. Place the trivet in the multi-cooker and pour water into the pot up to trivet level. Place the cake pan on the trivet.

Secure the lid in place and set to Manual or High Pressure for 50 minutes. At the end of cooking, use the NPR method (see page 4). Leave to cool, then pop in the fridge for an hour before serving. Dust with cinnamon just before serving.

# BANANA RICE PUDDING

1 tablespoon butter
500 ml/2 cups almond
    or coconut milk
110 g/scant $^2/_3$ cup pudding rice
    (you can use Arborio rice, too)
2 tablespoons maple syrup, plus
    extra to serve if you wish
$^1/_8$ teaspoon ground nutmeg
$^1/_4$ teaspoon ground cinnamon
2 ripe bananas, peeled and
    sliced on the diagonal

Serves 4

*This is a deliciously 'creamy' dessert made without dairy. The banana and cinnamon combine really well.*

Press the Sauté button on the multi-cooker and add the butter. When melted, add the milk and bring to the boil. Stir in the rice.

    Secure the lid in place and set to Rice for 12 minutes. At the end of cooking, use the QPR method (see page 4), but keep warm with the lid on for a further 15 minutes. Stir in the maple syrup, nutmeg, cinnamon and banana and leave for another 2 minutes, then serve.

# CHOCOLATE PLANTAINS

50 g/3$^1/_2$ tablespoons butter
    or coconut oil
25 g/1$^2/_3$ tablespoons coconut
    sugar
a pinch of salt
1 tablespoon raw cacao powder
2 whole, ripe plantains, peeled
    and sliced 2-cm/$^3/_4$-in. thick
1 tablespoon nut butter (ideally
    almond or cashew), to serve

Serves 4

*Plantain, a relative of the banana, make fantastic desserts. This recipe is inspired by a classic flavour combination. Cooking the plantains this way really does show them off at their best.*

Press the Sauté button on the multi-cooker. Add the butter or coconut oil, coconut sugar, salt and cacao powder, plus 25 ml/scant 2 tablespoons water to the pot. Heat for a couple of minutes, then stir in the plantain slices to coat in the sauce.

    Secure the lid in place and set to Manual or High Pressure for 3 minutes. At the end of cooking, use the QPR method (see page 4). Serve with a good dollop of almond or cashew butter over the top.

# POACHED PEARS IN GRAPE JUICE

150 ml/²/₃ cup red grape juice
40 g/3¼ tablespoons coconut
   sugar
1 cinnamon stick
2 cloves
2 ripe but firm pears, peeled,
   with their bottoms sliced off
   so they will sit upright
Greek or coconut yogurt,
   to serve

Serves 2

*I don't know about you, but I am sometimes put off making poached pears in wine partly because I don't want to waste wine on pears and partly because of the quantities of sugar added to the wine. So this is a dish created to harness the nutritional value of grapes but with less sugar and no wasted wine.*

Press the Sauté button on the multi-cooker and add the grape juice, sugar and spices. Heat until the sugar has melted and the sauce has reduced a little. Add the peeled pears to the pot.

Secure the lid in place and set to Manual or High Pressure for 7–8 minutes, depending on the size of the pears. At the end of cooking, use the QPR method (see page 4).

Serve with Greek or coconut yogurt.

# CARROT CAKE

**CAKE**
95 g/scant ½ cup coconut sugar
140 g/10 tablespoons butter, softened
200 g/1½ cups grated carrot
1 teaspoon ground cinnamon
2 eggs
2½ teaspoons baking powder
135 g/1 cup wholemeal/whole-wheat spelt flour

**FROSTING (OPTIONAL)**
200 g/scant 1½ cups icing/confectioner's sugar
50 g/3 tbsp butter, at room temperature
200 g/scant 1 cup cream cheese

15-cm/6-in. diameter round non-stick springform cake pan

Serves 8

*Who doesn't love a carrot cake? This recipe produces a moist and sweet cake that is hard to resist.*

Mix all the cake ingredients together in a bowl. Pour the batter into the cake pan and place on the trivet. Add 450 ml/scant 2 cups water to the multi-cooker and lower the trivet and pan into the inner pot.

Secure the lid in place and set to Manual or High Pressure for 30 minutes. At the end of cooking, use the NPR method (see page 4) for 15 minutes, then use the QPR method. Be careful when you remove the lid not to drip any liquid onto the cake – if necessary, use a paper towel to dab excess water off the cake.

For the frosting, beat the icing/confectioner's sugar and butter together in a stand mixer (or use a handheld electric whisk). Add the cream cheese and beat until fully combined. Once the cake is cool, spread the frosting in a thick layer over the top.

# BANANA OAT SPONGE CAKES

a little oil, such as coconut oil, or melted butter, for greasing
2 bananas, peeled
2 eggs
120 g/1¼ cups gluten-free rolled/old-fashioned oats
100 ml/⅓ cup almond milk
¼ teaspoon baking powder
½ teaspoon ground cinnamon
40 g/2¾ tablespoons date nectar or maple syrup
cream or Greek yogurt, to serve

4 ramekins

Makes 4

*Oats are rich in fibre and are actually higher in protein than many other grains. These little cakes are a really tasty and substantial dessert. They are best eaten soon after cooking.*

Using a pastry brush, brush the insides of the ramekins evenly with the oil or melted butter. In a food processor, mix all the ingredients except the cream or yogurt together to form a thick batter. Pour an equal amount of the batter into each ramekin. Put 500 ml/2 cups water into the multi-cooker. Put the trivet in the pot and place the ramekins on top (two in the 6-litre pot or four in the 8-litre pot).

Secure the lid in place and set to Manual or High Pressure for 1 minute. At the end of cooking, use the NPR method (see page 4) for 5 minutes, then the QPR method. Remove the ramekins and run a knife around the edge of each to release the cakes, or serve them in the ramekins. These are best eaten warm, straight from the pot, with cream or Greek yogurt.

# ALMOND CHOCOLATE BROWNIE CAKE

100 g/scant ¾ cup plain/
  bittersweet chocolate, broken
  into squares
100 g/7 tablespoons butter
70 g/5²/₃ tablespoons coconut
  sugar
100 g/1 cup ground almonds
3 eggs
fresh raspberries, to serve

15-cm/6-in. round non-stick
  springform cake pan

Serves 6

*This is a deliciously moist chocolate brownie cake made without any grain-based flours.*

Melt the chocolate and butter in a medium saucepan over a gentle heat. Once melted, add the sugar and stir to combine. Stir in the ground almonds and then leave to cool.

In a separate bowl, beat the eggs until fluffy. Gently fold the eggs into the cooled chocolate mixture and pour into the cake pan. Pour 250 ml/ 1 cup water into the multi-cooker. Put the trivet into the pot, then place the cake pan on top.

Secure the lid in place and set to Manual or High Pressure for 12 minutes. At the end of cooking, use the QPR method (see page 4). Remove the cake pan and trivet from the pot and leave the cake to cool a little. If necessary, remove any drips of water on the surface of the cake with paper towels.

Serve at room temperature with fresh raspberries on the side.

# GLOSSARY

**Barbecue Sauce** – try to find one without added sugar.

**Coconut Aminos** – this is a soy-free alternative to soy sauce or tamari. Some coconut aminos taste very sweet. The ideal one is a salty-tasting sauce that can be used in place of soy sauce or tamari for those who want to avoid soy products.

**Coconut Sugar** – while coconut sugar is still a sugar and therefore to be used sparingly, it raises blood sugar more slowly than white granulated sugar so is a preferred option. It's produced from the nectar of coconut flower buds. The buds are cut open and the sap is captured, and then boiled down.

**Fish Sauce** – there are many brands on the market. I recommend using one without added sugar.

**Stevia** – this sugar alternative comes in powder form and is derived from the stevia leaf. It is reported to have no effect on blood sugar levels. You need to use such small amounts of this powder to sweeten foods that it is a useful and cost-effective natural sweetener to use in dessert recipes.

**Stock Paste** – there are many recipes in this book that call for stock cubes or stock paste. You are welcome to use either. I prefer stock paste because that way I know what's gone into the stock. There's a recipe for vegetable stock paste on page 31.

**Tamari** – this is gluten-free soy sauce.

**Tomato Ketchup** – try to find a reduced sugar or no added sugar version.

# INDEX

# ACKNOWLEDGEMENTS

This book wouldn't have been possible without the help of my incredible literary agent who sees opportunity in unexpected places. Jane Graham-Maw was ready to support me in my endeavours to build on my previous book and provide more quick and simple real-food meal solutions for busy people.

Maria Bravo got me hooked on my Instant Pot® with her inspiring and encouraging social media posts. Subsequently, Maria has been very supportive of me while I worked to produce

and test healthy recipes for the Instant Pot®.

To my recipe testers – Maria Bravo, Kate Hart, Alli Wiltshire, Pat Duckworth and June Bailey – thank you for your help and guidance, as well as testing and advising on recipe tweaks.

Finally, to my family who have enjoyed the experience of tasting lots of different meals each day, be that in the evenings or the next day in their lunchboxes. They are so incredibly supportive and have been great company during those long hours spent testing recipes in the kitchen.